The Post-COVID School

Grace Under Pressure

Dr. Nick Sutton

EduMatch
PUBLISHING

Chapter Authors

Dr. Nick Sutton (Chapter 1)
Holly Williams (Chapter 2)
Dr. Georgie Koenig (Chapter 3)
Carly Spina (Chapter 4)
Dr. Tina Halliman (Chapter 5)
Sara Bates (Chapter 6)
Jessica Donaldson (Chapter 7)
Dene Gainey (Chapter 8)
Jennifer Leban (Chapter 9)
Ben Dickson (Chapter 10)
Matt Jacobson (Chapter 11)
Brian Bates (Chapter 12)
Ben Sondgeroth (Chapter 13)
Dr. Kimako Patterson (Chapter 14)
Kyle Anderson (Chapter 15)
Dr. Lloyd Kilmer (Chapter 16)

Copyright © 2023 by Nick Sutton
Published by EduMatch®
PO Box 150324, Alexandria, VA 22315
www.edumatchpublishing.com

These books are available at special discounts when purchased in quantities of 10 or more
for use as premiums, promotions fundraising, and educational use. For inquiries and details,
contact the publisher: sarah@edumatch.org.

ISBN: 978-1-959347-24-8

Contents

Introduction

Illustration by Audrey Sutton

"Is this COVID stuff really serious enough to have schools closed?" This was the exact text message that I sent to a fellow superintendent in March 2020. Even as I sent it, I felt a little nervous. I honestly thought that the response I would receive would be met with a layer of condemnation, with me asking something so silly. I thought that perhaps even contemplating that this could happen would be ridiculous. However, as everyone now knows, this question was not only realistic, but it ended up being more accurate than we ever anticipated.

As I reflect upon my career, I have reached a point where I feel comfortable assessing and identifying what is effective teaching. Now I use the term "effective teaching" very purposefully because I prefer that term a lot more than "good teaching." While I can acknowledge that this is just maybe my perspective, I always felt that the term effective correlates to objectivity and the term good relates to subjectivity.

Objectivity in public education is important because it opens the door for so many conversations on topics on how to improve. I can connect so many new initiatives I hear about in public education with also having real data-driven targets to signify if the new initiative ever even had any kind of actual impact. When an educator is asked how something went, the response, "It went well," shouldn't be enough.

I am not entirely sure why the field of education is this way. It would be hard, if not impossible, to imagine this type of reality in other career fields. Could you imagine being an employee within the business field and when your boss asks how many items you sold, having your response be something similar to, "Quite a few. It went awesome." A business owner would want to know the exact figures. They would want actual data to determine success. The field of education should be no different.

Depending Too Much on Culture

A positive climate is so important for any successful school setting. I think at this point everyone knows that, but I sometimes fear that there is a reality of being too focused only on culture. I am fearful of making this comment because I see the endless ways that it could be misinterpreted negatively. I truly understand and advocate the value of a positive climate. However, the focus of an educational leader has to be more than just this. An educational leader has to be someone that wants to, and can, improve instructional practices.

When I began my administrative career, I was excited but also overwhelmed like anyone new entering this field. I was motivated and determined, and most definitely willing to put in whatever level of work ethic was necessary to make an impact. However, I became way too infatuated with only focusing upon improving and building a positive climate to the detriment of improving instruction.

It's interesting now as I reflect because it was certainly not as if I did not have an interest in curriculum and instruction. I enjoyed discussing teaching techniques and enjoyed dialogue revolving around curricular resources. Interestingly, for reasons I am still not entirely sure of, I was a new principal infatuated with the notion that a positive culture and climate would fix any and every problem. In other words, I truly thought this type of approach was the silver bullet for public education.

Needless to say, my thought process that focusing on a school's atmosphere would somehow be a correlational solution to every other challenge, including increasing student achievement, was not solidified. Perhaps more importantly though for my professional growth was the realization that it may be a part of human nature to search for the magical, easy solution before taking a metaphorical deep breath and acknowledging to ourselves that nothing in life worth improving is ever that easy.

At one point in my adult life right after college, in particular, I was not very healthy physically. I think I was the same as many other people in similar situations in that I tried a lot of different approaches before being successful in becoming healthier. These included crash diets, weird diets, and then no diets, while just hoping something would magically change with my waistline and mindset. It wasn't until I simply made the conscious decision to eat better, eat less, and jog each morning that I became a lot happier.

What is interesting about this process, as I now reflect many years later from the start of this transition, is that the solution was not a solution that I was not aware of. I knew becoming healthier would take effort and an actual change involving commitment and substance. I just wasn't in a place where this was a change I was ready to make. Now, I completely realize that weight loss for everyone is not always this simple, and I am certainly aware that my comparison does not apply to everyone reading this book. Instead, I want to make the point that for many of the challenges we all find in life, it is not that we do not know the solution to solve the problem. Instead, we are just not ready to do what it takes to improve.

Public Education

There are endless books discussing the topic of public education, and each has its merit and purpose. Some educational books provide beautiful and inspiring stories that are so motivating that it is what is needed to make us excited to go to the school we serve the next day. These types of books have tremendous value, but similar to my early administrative perspective that a positive culture and climate are all that is needed, these types of books cannot be the only type of improvement that an educator exposes themselves to. In other words, it would have been similar to me only hearing success stories about weight loss without actually committing to a plan of substance aimed at achieving the actual goal.

There has been an explosion of research related to the field of education over the last few decades, and this simple fact does not get the credence that it simply should. There needs to be a collective shift in thinking. Specifically, when an educator says, "I don't know what to do," it should be replaced by, "I don't yet know the existing solution to this issue."

There is action research available to almost every scenario in our field, and if the conclusion is then applied to the challenge an educator finds themself within, the question then becomes whether or not it is done with fidelity. The notion of a school, staff, or student body somehow being so unique that broad, existing research does not apply needs to become a false notion.

The Purpose of This Book

Every state has its beginnings for its system of public education, but one of the earliest was in 1647 when Massachusetts passed the Old Deluder Satan Act. While a bit more complicated than my summary, this legislation required all parents to ensure their children were able to read, so in response, towns supported teachers for their children. In this setting, instruction was based upon a teacher instilling knowledge directly to the student themselves at a pace and manner led by the teacher. This model, in many ways, has not deviated for the last three hundred years.

Currently, teachers find themselves in a strange new world in which students have more autonomy on what to learn, where to learn, and if they choose to learn in these remote or hybrid learning environments. We, as educators, are living through the next phase of public education. Schools are already beginning to evolve, and the pace at which it is happening is being expedited more than it ever naturally would have been.

The true impact of COVID-19 on public education will likely not be fully known or understood for decades. However, no one can reasonably take the position that it will not have some type of impact immediately. The term remote instruction, for example, went from a futuristic and bizarre concept to instead a term that even kindergarteners were aware of in a manner of months. Our society's expectations for public education are now different and based upon this.

What is critical is that we as public educators tap into and depend on research-driven best practices in the situation we now find ourselves in more than ever before. For example, whether or not someone is in the field of education, they have experienced the ineffective and boring classroom approach of an instructor only lecturing about facts with the goal that they are then memorized by students. We have all lived through this type of setting, and no one will be shocked to learn there is no research that supports this, and yet it still happens.

There are also virtual classrooms right now that are set up with the best of intentions. They have fancy Bitmojis, interesting-looking online classrooms, and teachers that are doing their best. However, they greet their students each day through a live video call in which they then lecture for forty-five minutes. Students are then tasked to take this information into memory even though all of it could also be found through a simple internet search engine. We then wonder as a society why students are not engaged. Most frustrating is that there is research that indicates what we should be doing instead, but this still isn't universally accepted.

While this is just one example, it is aimed at proving my point and the value of this book. Each chapter that follows is authored by an amazing individual in the field of education. Their backgrounds are varying and widely encompassing, and each author has a specific passion and strength. These passions and strengths have also been aligned to a topic, and each topic is then delved into for the benefit of every school trying to decipher what to do now to impact students from the lessons learned after COVID-19. Every educator that reads this book will find themselves naturally drawn to the chapter topic that most closely resembles their own area of expertise but will also find value in learning more about the impact this pandemic may have on other areas they may not have even considered. Each chapter will outline the best practices of an area of education, the anticipated impact of COVID-19, and then, most importantly, what recommendations a school should consider now moving forward.

Again, the research exists for virtually all of the challenges a school encounters when aimed at helping students reach their fullest potentials. Many times there is just not the inherent drive or need to change, even if there is data that indicates the need to do so. One positive from a worldwide pandemic may very well be that educators find themselves in a reality in which they do not have the choice anymore. They have to change because the world has changed. This book aims to provide a little guidance, advice, and help as we all now take on this new world together.

What Would You Do If Your House Burnt Down?

Sadly, I realized while dreaming up the concept of this book that I know more than a couple of people that have experienced their house burning down. Luckily, in every instance, no one was ever hurt or injured, but nonetheless, the mental impact of such an experience would be overwhelming. I strive for organization and order in my life to such a degree that I could not even fathom how difficult and devastating it would be to have my house burn down and lose all of my possessions.

However, I do think I would find a sense of comfort in knowing that I would get the opportunity to start from scratch in a sense. Now please do not misunderstand the point I want to make by interpreting my comparison as underplaying the utter tragedy and sense of loss from such an event. This could not be further from my intended direction. Instead, it is my goal for everyone reading this to put their mind in a place in which they can reflect on how they would start from a new beginning.

If you were going to rebuild your home, what would you do differently? New color? Different furniture? Change the location of a room?

If you are anything like me, you would begin to reach a point of bittersweet excitement. It would obviously be a horrific and stressful experience to go through a home being destroyed, but opportunities to start from a new beginning are not something that happen every day. It would be a chance to avoid past mistakes and to improve more than ever before.

In so many ways, public education's "house" burnt down in the spring of 2020 due to COVID-19. Public educators went from a world in which students all came and sat at desks, and we never imagined a reality that this would not be the case. Every teacher, principal, bus driver, paraprofessional, or any other staff member in a school district saw their "house" burn down. This was a scary and stressful experience and one that profoundly impacted us all. However, we now also find ourselves engaged in a once-in-a-lifetime experience and opportunity in our field. Similar to how we would be asking ourselves rhetorical questions if our actual house burned down, we now have the opportunity to ask ourselves how public education should be rebuilt.

What do we keep? What do we rebuild? Perhaps, most importantly, what practices should we throw out?

We certainly never asked or fathomed that we would be in the situation we find ourselves in. This applies not only to the field of public education but also to our society as a whole. However, we have a choice on whether or not this experience will ultimately be a tragedy or an opportunity. I ask that you elect this to be a beginning and see this book as a platform for dialogue, discussion, and reflection. Each chapter will discuss a topic in the area of education, how it has been changed, and most importantly, what should be considered for the future of a post-COVID-19 world.

No one has all of the answers now, but there is one thing for sure. The world and education have changed, and we now need to embrace and change with it.

Chapter 1
Embracing Change
Dr. Nick Sutton

Illustration by Jack & Olivia Morland

Introduction

There are times that I look out my office window and wonder how amazing it is that I am here. Currently, I find myself working as a superintendent in the Chicago, Illinois area. I really love being a superintendent. I really and truly do.

I think for me I enjoy being in a position in which decisions can be made instantly that will positively impact kids. I am no longer the person that has to sell the premise of a new idea to someone that ultimately makes the decision. I am the person that makes the decision, and I enjoy that. I sometimes see other schools become paralyzed to make a decision because the process gets lost among a bureaucratic system of endless committees and a climate of hesitation to do something new.

When making decisions, I strive to involve as many others as possible. By doing so, the final product always ends up being a better outcome than it ever would have been if I had just worked on the idea by myself in isolation. However, I do enjoy being the person that can just work hard to ensure some type of decision has been made. Decisions impact kids. Decisions move school districts forward.

Before becoming a school district superintendent, I rose through the ranks in the field of education like almost all other administrators do in that I started as a teacher, then a principal, and then transitioned to my current role as superintendent. As a teacher, I was unique in that I was never a teacher that ever totally fell in love with a specific content area. Instead, I was someone that realized I enjoyed instructing middle school-aged children and that was really all that mattered to me. I have my middle school teaching endorsements for language arts, math, science, and social studies, so I honestly was indifferent to which curriculum I was tasked to teach as long as it was in a sixth through eighth-grade classroom. This setting is where I knew I was at my best and also had the most fun.

This realization then naturally led to the beginning of my administrative career as a middle school principal. I had the privilege of leading two different schools while being a principal, and it was such a fun experience. Being a middle school principal is such a wonderful and unique job, and it prepared me to feel comfortable working in a setting in which wearing many different hats is the norm.

After a while, I found myself wanting more. I think most educators that climb the ladder of administration in the field of education have this type of trait. I enjoy new challenges and am at my happiest when I have a nice balance of work demands that stretch me to my professional limits. It was this foundation that brought me into becoming a school district superintendent. As a superintendent, I have held a few different positions at this point in my career. Specifically, I have been in a very rural setting, and now, with my current positions being so very close to Chicago, it is the complete opposite.

Originally growing up in a small farm town in southeast Iowa, it has been a fun and unexpected ride. At one point I can recall being so desperate and excited to land that first teaching job. I laugh at myself now because of how many different opportunities I have been fortunate enough to have experienced. Ultimately, I have not seen another field that is as satisfying as the field of education though. Teachers, principals, and superintendents get to impact lives in everything that they do. Waking up every morning and remembering that each day comes with that possibility is something I am still absolutely drawn to.

The Traditional Change Process in Public Schools

I was so naive as a beginning teacher. I see that now and see it clearly, but I definitely did not see it that way as I was finishing up my student-teaching experience. As a student-teacher, I was so focused on succeeding, and even just surviving, within the classroom that I think I was oblivious of other aspects of the school going on outside of me.

I wanted to fine-tune my teaching strategies and figure out how I could ensure a room full of twenty-five eighth graders paid attention to me, that I never had the time or inclination to really see what was happening, good or bad, throughout the rest of the school. Now, as I reflect, I had the awareness that some teachers were better than others, and some programs were successful, and others were not. I knew what was working well, and also what parts were areas that had room for improvement. What never occurred to me was why various aspects of the school were the way they were.

As I transitioned into my teaching career, it was then that I began to notice some trends and also garner some realizations. One specific instance that comes to mind for a setting that I taught at was the practice of team teaching. For those that are unfamiliar with this concept, it essentially refers to the practice of combining two separate classrooms into one larger one, where the two teachers work collaboratively to instruct both classes at the same time. The premise is that one teacher would lead full-class instruction while the other teacher would work with struggling students as needed.

Like many new ideas, I am sure this one seemed like it had merit when originally considered. It's not that I can't acknowledge that the practice seems like it could be impactful if done correctly. Think about it. A student is being taught while there are two teachers available if the child needs assistance. That fact alone would make it seem like a concept worth considering. However, like so many new initiatives, I wonder if the actual follow-through is lost because the new idea is never done with any fidelity. Instead, simply implementing the idea is considered enough.

When I was a classroom teacher early in my career, I had the unique combination of extreme objectivity and also a drive to want to do whatever was best to impact kids. These traits were essentially driven by the fact that I had so little experience and didn't know any better. This trait was then probably unique because it impacted me both positively and also negatively. I can still clearly recall seeing these team-taught classrooms where one teacher would use poor instructional strategies of predominant lecturing to try and engage approximately sixty students while the other teacher was just sitting at their desk letting the other take their turn to "have to" teach.

As I reflect, I do feel like it was positive that I had the instructional knowledge of best practices and the inherent drive to want to help students that I knew this team-teaching approach was poor. However, my lack of experience also definitely made me someone that was woefully unaware of how what was best for kids was not always enough of a variable to suggest a change. It was this experience that made me first learn just how much change is sometimes resisted in schools. I went to the administration of the school to share my concerns and the valid reasons that this team-teaching approach was hurting students, and something that I felt frustrated and disheartened to be a part of. I had data and research to support my position, and although I was truly prepared to be told that they did not agree with me, what ended up happening was an outcome I was not prepared for. The administration knew the practice was ineffective, but was not interested in pursuing a significant change to avoid disturbing the solidified school culture of team teaching.

This experience, now many years later, is still one that is well imprinted into my memory, and also one that solidified a significant realization I still have to this day. A poor practice that is not effective is not enough to change if there are enough influential staff members that do not want it to. Now why this is this way can be due to several different variables and factors. It could be impacted by weak administration, a climate that doesn't emphasize research, self-centered staff that care more about the ease of their day regardless of students to name a few, or educators that may have good intentions but just do not know a better way.

In so many ways, though, the reasons for how the situation for my example came to be doesn't even matter. There was a poor practice in place that was detrimental to kids. Based upon this, every staff member could be placed into one of two generalized categories. Category one would be some of the staff members that were oblivious that this practice was so poor, and category two would be the staff members that knew this was a poor practice, but for whatever reason, did not feel compelled to see it change. It is this lack of drive to want to improve I find fascinating.

There are a lot of examples for change models out there, and even if an educator is familiar with none of them, they will realize that change doesn't happen easily. People naturally get accustomed to their routines, and if there isn't a reason to do something different, then many times it just does not happen. There has to be a widely accepted reason that is established by an educational leader to begin the process of anything transitioning to something different.

According to Kotter (2008), successful change efforts have to begin with a leader evaluating an entity's current situation objectively and then taking some type of bold action to create the necessary sense of urgency to change. Having a good idea is simply not enough to create action for something to be different. There has to be a collectively felt need shared amongst the staff.

I wholeheartedly believe that traditional change is entirely dependent on this variable. Despite the different definitions, change begins when there is a broadly accepted need to do so. As I reflect many years later, this is what was lacking in my example above. No one besides me truly saw any inherent reason to change the practice. It didn't matter that there was no research to support it. It didn't matter that there was no data to show that it was working. It didn't matter that the practice wasn't even being done correctly. All that mattered was that no one saw enough of a reason to create a sense of urgency to deviate.

This application of illogical thinking has been historically utilized in public education. Any individual can walk into a school and notice some ineffective practices. Take, for example, the instructional practice of round-robin reading. This approach to learning is anything but engaging for children, and it does not require a well-educated school administrator to know this. However, in many school classrooms, this practice very much remains. There is no research to support it. No data indicates it is impactful. There is also a plethora of other engaging instructional practices that exist to replace it. So why does it continue to exist? There is no sense of urgency to change.

The Best Practices for Change

I am the first to admit that I certainly do not have everything figured out for implementing change in a public school. In fact, I will probably be spending the rest of my career trying to discover the perfect way to inspire others to follow my lead. There is research that exists on how to lead others towards something new, and when examining these approaches, I believe some commonalities do begin to surface.

Previously, I mentioned the work of John Kotter and his steps for bringing forth change. The basic outline and its definition are listed below (Kotter, 1996).

1 - Establish a sense of urgency - People will not change unless they see the reason to do so.
2 - Create a guiding coalition - Building a group to lead the change.

3 - Develop a vision and strategy - Create a vision defining the change.
4 - Communicate the change vision - Tell everyone about why the change is happening.
5 - Empower broad-based action - Involve others in the change effort.
6 - Generate short-term wins - Recognizing the work being done by people working towards the change.
7 - Consolidate gains and produce more change - Create momentum by building on initial successes of the new change.
8 - Anchor new approaches in the corporate culture - Ensuring that the new change becomes a part of the institutional practices, so it never goes away.

Change is Systematic

I think one of the primary reasons I have always believed in and remember this particular change process is that I can envision specific examples I recall living through when contemplating the success or failure of a particular change I led throughout my career. Take step four from the list above, for example. It refers to communicating with staff and stakeholders why something new is being considered. While this may seem obvious at first, it isn't always the norm.

While there are certainly examples that come to mind of failed changes that I observed, I can also certainly think of failed changes that were also under my leadership. One particular experience was when I was still a principal. This story begins with establishing that I love the practice of peer walkthroughs for teachers. I never understood why building leaders do not push more for teachers to never instruct solely in isolation. If a school is going to have a climate of instructional collegiality, then I am not sure how that can happen without teachers observing other teachers to then be a catalyst to discuss what they see.

Regardless, I was desperately trying to build this type of climate at the principal position I was in. I had begun the process of professional development on conducting peer walkthroughs and their purpose. Then I worked with some building leaders on how we could create a system of teachers watching other teachers instruct and an eventual vision of what this would look like. In other words, I had successfully followed the first three steps of Kotter's (1996) process. It was not continuing with his process that the change implementation went off course.

After explaining the reasoning and getting initial buy-in for the change, I then immediately implemented the change and then slowly observed (to my dismay) it did not go particularly well. I got impatient and never globally communicated what the ultimate vision was to the entire staff of why this was happening. To this day, this is why I still believe the practice of peer walkthroughs at this particular school never was solidified and became an eventual concrete institutionalized practice. I had just assumed the initial buy-in and interest would be enough.

It was based upon this experience that I learned change is systematic. The change will not just happen organically. It will not just happen by chance. Instead, it occurs because of purposeful action.

Timing is Everything

Maxwell (2007) has a pretty widely known list of leadership laws that apply to virtually any industry. However, the one law of leadership that he identifies that relates to my example described above is the law of timing. What this law essentially describes is for a leader to not only be able to see a situation, but to know whether it makes sense to implement the new practice now or at a different time. The right action at the right time is wonderful, but in turn, the right action at the wrong time can be a complete disaster.

I am a person that believes in research and truly gets frustrated when educators spend inordinate amounts of time either ignoring data or being apprehensive to take action to address a need. In my mind, there are so few, if any, problems that exist in public education that cannot be addressed through some existing conclusions of previous research. However, I have also realized that a good idea will be trumped by bad timing every time.

I honestly think most issues that need to be addressed in public schools are not difficult to identify. We live in a world where so much information can be discovered about a school with a simple internet search engine query. Any one of us, regardless of whether we are even an educator, can find general information about a school district online and then identify concerning pieces of data.

The difficulty when it comes to school improvement is taking those initial and crucial first steps that it is no longer defensible to be accepting of practices that do anything short of positively impacting kids. While I acknowledge that there are always a variety of variables that make school improvement a challenge, not for the weak of heart, establishing a sense of urgency is paramount (Kotter, 2008), but not always easy. However, since everything we have previously known to be within public education has been disrupted, challenged, and even destroyed due to COVID, perhaps now is the universal sense of urgency we all need to deal with achievement gaps, poor student performance, and social-emotional needs with a sense of renowned determination that has never been possible before.

Change Can Be a Contagious & Positive Mindset

I sometimes think individuals forget their core purpose. It isn't planned. It isn't something that is done purposefully. It is something that just happens. However, this does occur, and we have to acknowledge this.

People that decide that they want to be an educator do so because of some type of personal core value or purpose in which they want to impact others. I have heard this basic premise described and summarized in several different ways, but the overall idea remains the same. A future educator wants to enter this type of field because they want to help.

What I have learned during my own career experiences is that this foundational principle is sometimes disrupted, if not lost. Having said that, the reasons that this happens may not be for reasons that are not understandable.

The Impact of COVID-19

As I write this section of my chapter, I still marvel at how profound and ongoing the impact of COVID-19 appears to be on public education. I remember in January 2020 vaguely hearing in passing while listening to the news about this weird new virus but thinking that this would never be something significant. I can recall around March 2020 thinking that states would never close down schools once rumors about this began circulating.

I then firmly believed that schools would never be closed longer than a couple of weeks around April 2020 when the shutdowns finally occurred. Every time I made a personal prediction about everything related to COVID-19, I underestimated it and underestimated it badly.

While I obviously misjudged COVID initially, I am sure other educators foresaw the significance much better and much quicker than I did. What does seem pertinent and necessary at this time is to acknowledge that COVID was and is a big deal, and with any big deal, it correlates to change. While the changes may or may not be welcomed, change is here, and it is here to stay.

Make Change Purposeful

It isn't easy changing. Whether the change is personal, professional, or anything in between, it is not easy to begin doing something differently. Then, taking into consideration when the change is being forced upon you, it becomes anything but welcomed. However, if any of us are in a situation that is largely outside of our control, we need to force ourselves to reflect and realize what variables are still at least within our control.

I ask anyone to now recall a recent difficult situation that they encountered in their life. We have all had them, and it is just a part of life itself. No matter what detrimental personal experience anyone reading this right now is imagining, it is no doubt a situation that occurred at least partly, if not largely, due to reasons that you did not have control over. While going through a challenging time is difficult enough, it becomes even more cumbersome when someone realizes that a large portion of the experience is due to variables we have no control over. These types of situations warrant feelings of being overwhelmed and possibly even feelings of hopelessness.

I have found that when any of us are encountering a situation like this, if we look hard enough, we all realize that there are details that we do have control over. I genuinely feel like this realization is the first step to working through difficulties, and then coming out in a better position than you ever would have without this type of thought process. COVID-19 is outside of our control. However, how we embrace this experience and choose purposeful change is within our control.

The most prolific position that I can take when suggesting interventions to support children and schools is to acknowledge and never forget that there is established research for any recommendation an educator could come up with. Educators need to use this research, and not allow for subjective opinions or thought processes to enter the discussion. While this point may be simplistic, it really should be to create a point of emphasis.

Take into consideration summer school as a remediation tool for students that are behind. I cannot count how many times I hear about schools thinking this type of intervention will be how they can address poor performance. It's fascinating to me because there are so many school interventions that are done because they are the interventions that are simply always done. There is little, if any, thought as to whether or not the intervention being considered will work.

According to Hattie (2009), sending students to summer school will likely not make much of a difference. His research indicates that unless the summer school program is specifically tailored to students' needs and parents are heavily involved, the positive attributes are likely to be slight or not at all. However, interventions such as summer school are well known, and well-known interventions seem to be suggested due to their almost universal awareness. Sadly, though, my experience has been that suggested interventions are seldom based solely on their correlation to research.

If we as educators know that students are going to need learning loss addressed due to COVID, why should we assume past practice interventions that had little impact will be any different now? Change must be purposeful, and purpose can only be found when it is based upon tangible ideas that have merit.

Final Thoughts

I knew of so many schools, directly and indirectly, that leaped forward with their technology utilization when the reality of an educational atmosphere in which students learn remotely became a reality. Teachers began using online classroom platforms rather than chalkboards. Administrators began ordering Chromebooks rather than textbooks. Districts began creating scenarios that learning took place when the student wanted to engage rather than necessitating it take place only from 8 am to 3 pm.

These were positive changes, and while the pace of these changes was nothing we asked for, they happened. The key now at this point is to not go backward. Society mirrors public education in that it always keeps moving forward and evolving. COVID-19 simply made this pace expedite at a speed none of us expected or wanted. While recovering from this unwelcome experience, educators must realize that devolving to the way things were before COVID is not a healthy coping strategy, or even possible at this point. Education has changed, and embracing this change is in many ways everyone's only positive choice.

Chapter 2
The Role of a School Library

Holly Williams

Illustration by Anderson Williams

Introduction: Why a Librarian?

I had just passed the salt down the table when my cousin blurted out, "Why do you want to be a librarian? Where is the job security? Aren't printed books a thing of the past when we have the internet?" The room stilled as all eyes turned on me in eager anticipation of an answer.

I responded then, as I still respond to these questions today, "As long as there is a pursuit for knowledge, I will have a job." A librarian's purpose is not simply to arrange books on a shelf and be up to date on the newest novel. A librarian is an advocate for information. Information is not just printed, it comes in various forms: electronic, video, sound, music, images, art, and so much more! Information is always evolving. The role of a librarian is to organize that information, to make it accessible to everyone. It's a never-ending cycle of discovery and creation.

For the last fifteen years, I have worked in libraries. Though I loved being in the public library, I knew after student teaching in a middle school that I wanted to be in a classroom more. My first year as a school librarian was a challenge. Like many first-year teachers, I came into the position excited and full of amazing ideas. And like many first-year teachers, I quickly learned the challenges that I faced. Tight budgets, leaky walls, and bookshelves from the 1960s presented some physical obstacles. But the hardest one to overcome was changing the definition of the library.

Like my family, I quickly learned many people did not have the same definition of a school library as I did. I had studied English Language Arts as an undergraduate and attained my endorsement to teach grades sixth through twelfth. This foundation gave me a unique perspective in graduate school. As I sat in classes learning about administration, cataloging, and programming, I was excited to see everything a school librarian could do to supplement the classroom. School libraries are full of great materials that can help students to grow emotionally and intellectually. When this information is utilized properly, every child has a chance to succeed. As a librarian, I could help teachers and students unlock this power.

Over the years, I learned how to foster relationships with my colleagues. Book fairs, reading incentive programs, and book talks are all essential parts of growing excitement for reading. But my favorite part of being a school librarian is guiding a new generation of learners in the process of discovery and creation. Collaborating with teachers on research projects has always been my greatest joy. All of our projects were a journey of locating information to analyze, use, and publish our findings. Together in science, my seventh graders created audio recordings about different exotic animals. We then uploaded these to the internet and made them accessible through QR codes. You can visit a wildlife park in Arcola, Illinois today and scan these QR codes to hear a student tell you about the animals right before your eyes. In eighth grade, our students discussed the misconceptions of women's roles in history. They each created a children's book of an unsung American heroine and then read these books to Kindergarteners. Again in eighth grade, students read historical fiction in Reading, in Social Studies they learned about the true events these books were set in, and for English, they wrote news stories highlighting the characters and events as if they were journalists from the actual era.

In all of these situations, I found myself working alongside teachers that had some amazing ideas but just needed a little help to get there. My expertise in how to navigate and use the information and their expertise in content allowed us to create a learning environment where students grew in knowledge and creativity.

How Libraries Have Been Traditionally Viewed: Quiet and Pristine

To reach this shared vision, I had to help rewrite some traditional thinking. So let's be honest, watch any movie, read any book, or search for a librarian meme and what do you get? A room full of books, where people are studying diligently, it's quiet, and everything has its place. To cap it off, the whole facility is overseen by a little old lady in a cardigan, glasses on a chain, shushing anyone who breathes too loudly. There are locations in the world that fit this description. How else would we get the stereotypes, am I right? Yet in all my years of working in education, I can count the number of times I've observed this type of school library on one hand.

Instead, I have found libraries to be the central hub of activity and flexibility within schools. Maker spaces or STEAM labs are frequently housed in the library. The space to spread out access to information makes school libraries the ideal place to brainstorm and test new ideas. Collaboration spaces, flexible seating, computer labs, and charging stations are commonly found in school media centers because they are the perfect place for people to congregate. I once got a complaint from teachers that the library was too noisy before school. Ideas grow and thrive in the right environment. If I had shushed my students, I would have created a roadblock to this growth. Not to mention affecting their social-emotional needs. So, we compromised. I changed the space and flow of traffic to make room for quiet study areas and more social meeting spaces. Thus meeting the needs of those that needed less distraction to study, and those that needed social connections to emotional growth.

Over the years, the term for a school library has changed to a *media center*. According to the Merriam-Webster Dictionary online, the root word of library is the Latin form for books. So perhaps changing the name to media center makes it more encompassing of what it truly is: an environment where information is cultivated, conveyed, and expressed (Merriam-Webster, n.d.). But changing a name is only one step in the process. It is an action that truly changes the mindset. Truly effective school libraries are "dynamic learning environments that bridge the gap between access and opportunity for all learners" (American Association of School Libraries [AASL], 2018).

I have had countless conversations with school librarians who are fighting to keep their jobs. Administration, faculty, and parents see the media specialist as a keeper of books only. Today, the frequency of media specialists being forced to move between buildings, teach classes outside of the library curricula, maintain technology, and still manage physical and digital collections on a limited budget is astounding. The truth is school media specialists are stretched too thin and our students are losing out.

Defining the Best Practices of the School Library

The stronger the school library program, the better students achieve. According to Gretes (2013), there have been over sixty impact studies in twenty-two states that conclude that well-equipped school libraries with full-time certified librarians and adequate support staff directly impact student learning. Building a successful library program takes the efforts of both the school media specialist and the administration. When the two work together, the entire learning community is positively impacted. Yet the best practices of a school media center are some of the hardest to achieve.

"Increased expenditure per student makes students perform better" (Gretes, 2013). Without a doubt, the best practice for a successful library program is adequate funding. It is essential to keep technology, online, and print resources up to date within the school media center. High-quality collections that have up-to-date information and high-interest literature build a library that is visited and used frequently. By providing access to an array of well-managed resources, school libraries enable academic knowledge to be linked to deeper, personalized learning (AASL, 2018). This is especially important for students impacted by poverty. The school library offers them access to resources they cannot afford and thus impacts their reading achievement (Gretes, 2013). It is universally proven the more you read, the more you learn. Yet, many collections are outdated and insufficient to meet the needs of their learning communities (Arp, 2003). When library budgets are made a low priority within a school, this has a ripple effect on student achievement. Adequate funding is only one piece in the puzzle. The research proves that schools with a full-time certified librarian achieve higher marks on test scores (Arp, 2003, Gretes, 2013). State certification requirements may vary slightly by state, but all share a common focus on information literacy. Certified librarians are trained in the skills of accessing, evaluating, and producing information. National and state library learning standards are rooted in information literacy. Certified librarians are the most equipped among a building's educational staff to teach these skills because they are masters at seeking information for any subject. When made a member of curriculum committees and allowed time to collaborate with teachers, certified librarians can listen to the information needs of their learning community and build a physical and digital information hub that supports classroom instruction and cultivates learning. There is so much information available in the world today; the quality of which varies drastically. The school librarian has the training to shift through this information and provide access to only the best. They can then teach others how to access and evaluate this information successfully over any subject focus. Information literacy doesn't happen overnight and needs to be taught over time and with consistency for students to be the most successful (Arp, 2003). AASL's position statement says it nicely, "School libraries staffed with state-certified professionals provide an approachable, equitable, personalized learning environment necessary for every learner's well-rounded education" (AASL, 2018). Yet finding a school library with full-time certified staff is hard to do.

Here in the state of Illinois, there are, as of 2021, only three universities that provide certification for school library endorsement, and only two of these institutes have a master's program. To receive your library endorsement from the state, in addition to your educational license, you must complete at least eighteen course credit hours and complete the Library Information Specialist test (ISBE, n.d.). The sheer cost of receiving this endorsement, along with the limited universities that offer a state-certified program, deters many teachers from pursuing this certification. There is no loan forgiveness for school media specialists, as the state labels them as support staff. Yet librarians have state learning standards, and many are required to submit student growth goals along with their professional evaluations. Finally, with the increasing need for technology within schools, the school media center has become a hub for tech support. This makes sense, as librarians are trained to be information gurus and technology is the number one avenue today in which information is accessed. However, this means more and more school librarians are being replaced by technology staff (Arp, 2003). We have all seen the drop in certified teachers over the last couple of years. The number of certified librarians is even smaller.

Certified librarians are not the only staff, however, needed within a successful library program. Adequately staffed libraries with support staff also have a direct impact on student achievement. Gretes mentions that in studies conducted in Pennsylvania and Colorado, libraries that were staffed by a full-time librarian and a full-time support person had students with 15% higher test scores than other schools with less staffing (2013). Library support staff make it possible to have more flexible scheduling for the library. There are a lot of day-to-day tasks that need to be done within the school media center to operate properly. The maintenance of the collection alone is time-consuming, as books need to be checked out, checked in, shelved, repaired, and processed. When these routine tasks are done by support staff, a school librarian is free to participate in instructional activities such as providing professional development for teachers, teaching information literacy lessons, and keeping up to date on technology (Arp, 2003). In addition, countless studies have proven that the more access students have to books, the better. By having a full-time support staff member in the library, the doors can be open for longer hours and there is no need to shut them due to lack of supervision. Flexible schedules and longer hours help students perform better (Gretes, 2013). The years that I had support staff with me in the school library for more than just lunch and planning made a huge difference in my ability to collaborate and teach. When the support was available, we were able to do more interdisciplinary units and create projects that connected our students to the real world. When the support was unavailable, I chose to stay in the media center instead of going into the classrooms. The studies by Gretes highlight that access to the media center has a positive impact on student achievement (2013). With no support staff to help oversee the library, my choice was to shut the doors, thus cutting off access, or stay and provide students with the resources they needed. It was a hard choice, but one that had to be made. The decision to assign support staff to the library is made by the administration. But funding is the driving force behind a district's ability to provide this valuable aspect of a successful library program.

In essence, if we want to provide our students with a more well-rounded education, we need to have stronger school libraries. Adequate funding for collection development, certified, full-time librarians, and support staff is the foundation of a good library program. Yet, the ultimate growth for student achievement depends on the ability of the school librarian to be an instructional leader.

How COVID-19 Has Impacted the Future of the School Library?

On August 16, 2021, editorial cartoonist Bramhall posted on the *New York Daily News* Facebook page a cartoon entitled "Meet the Warlords." (https://www.facebook.com/NYDailyNews/photos/meet-the-warlordssee-more-bramhall-editorial-cartoons-bitly3k4mmee/10158252601047541/). In this image, as the four horsemen of the apocalypse, War, Famine, Pestilence, and Death, ride into battle, they are joined by a new rider, Misinformation. This satirical cartoon brings to light a very real issue within our society. In a matter of milliseconds, we can access information via our phones. The biggest avenue for accessing and creating is social media. Where before it took days, weeks, or even years to publish a work, now it takes seconds to create and publish. Yet this information is not always respectful, thoughtful, or inclusive, nor is it always based on fact and reason. During COVID-19, and still today, we have seen an increase in misinformation. Facts are quickly being confused with opinion. And because of the overabundance of information, it is becoming increasingly easy to find sources, regardless of their validity, that support your argument. I had a group of middle schoolers trying to convince me that Helen Keller was a fictional character based solely on a TikTok video that had gone viral. Building the skills to evaluate and use information accurately is at a critical point today. And I would argue that we need more advocates of reliable information than we ever did before.

The state bill that was adopted in July 2021 by the Illinois General Assembly has come at an important turning point. 105 ILCS 5/27-20.08 section one clearly states (2021), "'media literacy' means the ability to access, analyze, evaluate, create, and communicate using a variety of objective forms, including, but not limited to, print, visual, audio, interactive, and digital texts." By the 2022-2023 school year, all public high schools within the state of Illinois are to adopt a unit on media literacy.

Luckily, information literacy is at the heart of library standards. In 2008, the Association of Illinois School Library Educators ([AISLE], 2018) published learning standards for K-12 libraries. These standards were approved and supported by the Illinois State Board of Education for the standard of teaching within school libraries. There are five areas of focus: 1) access information efficiently, 2) evaluate information critically, 3) use information accurately, creatively, and ethically, 4) appreciate literature and other creative expressions, and 5) understand and practice internet safety. Not only do the Illinois Standards Aligned Instruction for Libraries, more commonly known as I-SAIL, provide a blueprint for school librarians in their classrooms. These standards map out how library learning objectives support Illinois Common Core, Next Generation Science, National School Library, and ISTE standards for students. These standards of teaching are frequently revisited and updated, as the need for media literacy has increased throughout the years.

School librarians recognized early on that the growing use of technology was changing the way that information was accessed, analyzed, and created. The American Association of School Libraries recognizes the critical role certified librarians fill by providing instruction for information and digital literacy (AASL, 2018). These skills are not a one-and-done lesson either. Information literacy takes time to be taught and practiced across disciplines and platforms (Arp, 2003). By following library program best practices, we allow school librarians the opportunity to address the media literacy needs of our learners. Information literacy skills are an approach to information that bridges all disciplines. Whether you are researching a science project, exploring a historical event, writing an argumentative paper, or simply learning how to bake a cake, knowing how to access, evaluate, and use the information appropriately are valued skills.

By cultivating opportunities for school librarians to collaborate with teachers and not simply seeing them as additional tech support, we are building learning environments that help every child to succeed.

Final Thoughts: More Time Teaching

Though they are needed in the classroom more now than ever, librarians spend a majority of their time managing technology. During a recent conference in Champaign, Illinois, I heard countless librarians discussing how much of their time is spent managing student passwords, device repairs, and tech troubleshooting. This trend of technology takeover has been happening for years. In 2003, Arp noted that "school librarians often double as technology coordinators and staff technology trainers, and that in some cases, media specialists are simply being replaced by technology staff." It should not be surprising that school librarians are frequently looked to for their expertise in technology, as once again we are reminded that the most frequent access to information is via technology. But when that management of technology takes up so much time, the school librarian becomes increasingly isolated from faculty and thus the curricular needs of their learners. If we want to produce students that have strong information literacy skills, we must find the time to allow media specialists and teachers to collaborate and create course-integrated instruction and inquiry-based learning (Arp, 2003).

The evolution of information has only been heightened by the technology medium. And school libraries can help bridge those gaps between access and understanding when given a chance in the classroom. It's been years since that family dinner when my cousin questioned my career path. He is a retired school superintendent now and I would like to think that just maybe I was able to open his eyes a little. After all, it is my job to be an advocate of accurate information for all learners.

Chapter 3
The Impact on Reading Instruction

Dr. Georgie Koenig

Illustration by Teagan Koenig Jerz

Critical Definitions

E ven though this is a chapter about reading and the impact of COVID-19 on instruction, reading is part of an integrated system of skills. When we speak of individuals being literate or illiterate, it is related to their ability to read information and convey ideas or messages in writing. What is literacy? It is the act of reading and writing (Birsh & Carreker, 2018). Baker, Fien, Nelson, Pescher, Sayko, & Turtura (2017) provide a simple definition of reading. "Learning to read consists of developing skills in two critical areas: (1) Reading each word in texts accurately and fluently and (2) Comprehending the meaning of texts being read. This is known as the Simple View of Reading" (p. 1). Writing is a form of communication; in its basic sense, writing represents spoken language. Moats (2020) states "literacy teaching encompasses all major components of reading instruction and all layers of language. It develops students' ability to interpret and generate sound-spelling, syllables, morphemes, phrases, sentences, paragraphs and various genres of text" (p. 20). Therefore throughout this chapter about reading, the term literacy will also be used. Reading and writing work together as part of an effective and comprehensive instructional approach.

Introduction

"We remember events that elicit emotional reactions for a longer time than those that don't. The event is nearly always stamped with extra vividness, which results in enhanced memories" (Wolfe, 2010, p. 137).

On a beautiful late summer morning on the front lawn of my elementary school in the 1960s, I had such an emotional experience, I still remember the event with dramatic detail. It was the first day of the new school year. All of the children lined up behind their new teacher according to grade. Waiting patiently for everyone to get into line, I looked around at the other lines and that is when I spied Vivian in her dark colored paisley dress and long blonde hair standing in the kindergarten line. Being the overly helpful type, I became quite worried about Vivian's error.

I tapped Beth's shoulder who happened to be standing next to me and had been in the same kindergarten class as Vivian and me. "Beth, look Vivian is in the wrong line. Do you think I should let the teacher know?"

"No," replied Beth. Then, very quietly, she whispered to me, "Vivian is in the correct line. She has to repeat kindergarten because she didn't pass."

Fear gripped me as I looked in horror at poor Vivian in the kindergarten line. I didn't even know that it was possible to be held back. On that bright sunny day standing on the lush green lawn of the school, my worst fear came into the world.

Every school year I worried, "Would this be the year that I didn't pass?" My first-grade progress reports didn't help matters; they only intensified the fear. Despite my best efforts, I struggled to learn to read. The learning process was a mystery I just couldn't solve.

My confusion of how reading, spelling, and writing worked went on for years until one day my whole world changed.

On the last day of fifth grade, my dad told the family that we were moving to Texas for his new job. The move to Dallas provided the catalyst I needed to change the trajectory of learning failure. Thanks to a summer of reading because I didn't know anybody and a fantastic teacher, Mrs. Booker at Tom C. Gooch Elementary School, I began to solve the mystery of learning. When I moved back and began middle school, my reading placement had changed from the bottom reading group I'd been in before my move to the top enrichment reading group.

I know that if this life-altering move had not taken place, I would have continued down the path of being a poor learner. Research backs up my claim. As educators, we know that without effective intervention, students who are reading below grade level at the end of first grade continue to fall farther and farther behind their peers. For me this story represents several key points about the implications for post COVID-19 education:

- Emotional experiences shape who we are; the pandemic is such an event for all of us but especially for the school aged population.
- Even though the general public has sat in classrooms as students and seen movies about education does not necessarily mean many of them have a true understanding of what it takes to run and be an effective school. Teaching is not a simple or easy task. Research provides the numbers behind what educators face on a daily basis. Data from the United States Department of Education's National Center for Education Statistics (NAEP) has reported over the last decade that between 65% and 70% of U.S. students are not proficient in reading and writing, and this was before the pandemic. More resources, not fewer resources, are needed to tackle this issue. The pandemic has increased the need and urgency for support. However, educational systems cannot be guaranteed that additional resources will be available, therefore careful and critical decisions will need to be made about areas of greatest need.
- The disconnection between research in literacy (reading and writing) and classroom instructional practices have impacted students' abilities to meet proficient levels of performance. Students being out of school due to COVID-19 has further hindered the acquisition of adequate reading and writing skills.
- Teachers knowing about best practices and being able to effectively apply their knowledge is vital to improving student learning and results.

- The life outcomes of individuals leaving the K-12 system without being accomplished in reading and writing is grim.
- However, reading failure does not have to be a foregone conclusion; it can be prevented (Honig, 2001).

The importance and impact of these points as they relate to post COVID-19 reading instruction will be elaborated further.

Learning Journey and Reading Instruction

Why am I telling this story about my early learning journey? The experience shaped how I've operated as an educator. When working with students who, despite their desire and effort, are not seeing equivalent results in their reading acquisition, I remember what it was like to be in their place. As a result, I want to ensure students see themselves as capable learners. Therefore, the onus is on me to figure out how each student learns best. Additionally, once I entered the field of education in my desire to have students be successful learners, I have been on a quest for continuous professional betterment. Finally, the story reminds me that success is possible. In thinking of the future of education, I see parallels between my story of struggle to success in school to the current situation in education and COVID-19. The field of education has seen its own share of challenges and failures.

Professional Background

As an educator, I have seen districts and schools with more than 70% of their student body reading below a proficient level. Despite the best efforts of administrators and teachers, their students continue to not meet grade-level expectations. However, I believe COVID-19 can be the catalyst we need in education to change the lives of our students, especially those who find learning a challenge.

My professional career has provided me with a varied lens of viewing the challenges that we face as educators. Over the course of my more than thirty years in education, I have worked in three states, twenty-seven school districts, and over 150 different schools. I've seen learning from a teacher's perspective, from a learning consultant's viewpoint, as a professional developer, an administrator, and as a state interagency district improvement coach. Throughout my career, I've spent a large portion of it focused on reading achievement.

I've been fortunate enough to have led and been part of successful improvement initiatives resulting in significant changes in reading outcomes. Having the knowledge of what is possible, I have a firm conviction that as educators we can view the situation with COVID-19 as another death knell sounding the decay of our educational system or as a catalyst for what is possible and the building of a robust educational system.

As a country, we have had one of those epic moments that will mark all of us. In education, COVID-19 highlighted the gaping inequities in schooling our children and further intensified them. Teachers, administrators, and parents have worked with resolute determination over the last several decades to shore up the educational system to meet the ever-increasing needs of students and the decreasing resources. Again, they have met the current crisis with the same tenacious effort. After COVID-19 subsides, students, teachers, and administrators will return to school, but we will never be the same and education will be different in one form or another.

I believe we will have choices to make in reshaping our new reality. Will we continue down the obdurate path we've been on, or will we use COVID-19 as a launching pad for a better future for students and education as a whole?

"Together we stand at the threshold of galactic changes over the next few generations" (Wolf, 2018, p. 1). Which fork in the road will we choose to take? Will we take the well-worn road, or will we take the road of possibilities to something new and better?

Traditional View of Reading

The music cues up. On the large movie screen, a young teacher closes the classroom door and turns to face twenty-five fresh-faced children sitting in five rows, each row consisting of five individual desks. For the new teacher, winning these students over and teaching them to read and write will be a breeze. Of course, for cinematic dramatic effect, the teacher will encounter a few challenges that the teacher eventually creatively solves. The school year ends with the students being top-notch due to the teacher's fantastic tutelage. Cut to the final scene, it is the last day of the school year, and the students are cheering their teacher and saying how much they will miss the class. The final student leaves. The teacher shuts the classroom door and walks across the schoolyard to their car in the parking lot, gets in, and drives off with a satisfied smile. A job well done.

The movie scene is a common one. Most individuals recall similar settings as the ones depicted in education-based movies. Viewers could easily visualize themselves in the classroom reading round-robin, having the mandatory Friday spelling test, and turning in their written essays at the end of the day on the way out the door. Some will have pleasant memories of school and others will not have such happy thoughts about their experiences. However, almost no one would find the classroom scenes as foreign.

As much as the general population likes to think there is uniformity in schools in America, the reality is quite different than most individuals imagine. Inside the school, literacy instruction especially at the elementary level has been a dizzying array of content, pedagogy, and lack of clarity.

Historical Issues

Reading instruction has been plagued with confusion on what constitutes best practices (Chall, 1996). There historically has been a chasm between research and actual classroom practices. Bridging this crevasse of translating research into practice has been a daunting prospect. Typical drivers of instruction are publishing companies and philosophical camps on the best approach of how to teach reading. "Look and say" and "phonics" are two prominent methods of reading (Chall, 1996). Then, there is the variation on these two methods: basal readers, whole language, guided reading, and balanced literacy to name a few. Additionally, there is a variety of delivery techniques layered upon the different reading approaches.

It is no wonder teachers may not have a clear understanding of what constitutes best practices based on research. Playing into this lack of clarity are teacher preparation programs that sometimes provide incomplete or inaccurate information, lack of quality professional learning in the schools, and educational fads (Chall, 2000).

Historical Impact of Reading Practices

Confusion about best reading practices intensified during the reading wars of the '80s and '90s. The reading war occurred between two camps; the phonics group and the whole language group which had huge philosophical differences (Chall, 2000). The phonics group insisted that students must explicitly be taught forty-four phonemes to learn to read. Phonemes are the twenty-six letters and combinations of the letters (e.g., vowel teams, digraphs, etc.) or sounds used to create words. In their view, reading needed to be taught explicitly to children. In contrast to the whole language proponents' perspective, they believed literacy skills came as naturally as language does to children (Sherman & Ramsey, 2006). Further the whole language philosophy thought adults were confounding the acquisition of reading skills by being overly prescriptive and hindering children's learning (Goodman, 1986). As time went on, common ground could not be found. Instead, the two philosophical stances grew stauncher and more entrenched.

Two types of materials were used to implement these approaches to reading. Basal readers were and are commonly used for reading instruction. Traditionally, basal readers were associated with phonics. The whole language approach promoted the use of print, both fiction and nonfiction, using meaningful and relevant print found in a child's environment for reading instruction. It is important to know about these common approaches to reading to better understand current practices. The beliefs and instructional techniques of the past have influenced reading practices being used today. Some of those practices are effective. However, research found others ineffective. Knowing the pedagogical approaches supported by research assists in making quality educational decisions about teaching and learning.

As the reading wars raged on, students' reading scores began to decline. To calm the waters, Congress put the task of determining what the research said about what are the most effective methods and approaches to a National Panel of reading experts (NICHD, 2000). Before the report, reading arguments were based primarily on a philosophical viewpoint.

The Progression from Conflict and Confusion to Research Based Reading Practices

Basal Readers and Phonics

Reading materials with a long history are basal readers. The content of these instructional materials changed overtime based on current favored reading practices. Basal readers became more prominent and prescriptive as reading research from the 1960s was infused in the already existing basic basal. Many educators, parents, and students are familiar with the quintessential teacher's manual, student reading book, and workbook. Basals consisted of instructional materials arranged in a specific scope and sequence within each grade level and from grade to grade. The skills within the basal were delivered in a hierarchical manner from easiest to more challenging. The vocabulary in the readers and workbooks was highly controlled. Only previous and new learning skills, words, etc. were included in each new lesson. Basals were designed to be all-inclusive (Goodman, Shannon, Freeman, & Murphy, 1988).

Basal manuals provided everything a teacher needed to deliver the lessons. Some publishing companies emphasized the design ensured students learned how to read regardless of the teacher's skill level (Goodman, Shannon, Freeman, & Murphy, 1988). Presumably, the teacher only needed to follow the basal exactly as it was laid out. Some teachers complained about the explicit and directive manuals they had to follow, not allowing them to make instructional decisions (Chall, 2006). Unfortunately, the idea that reading failure would be eliminated or almost eliminated did not materialize. Teachers may or may not have followed the manual with fidelity, but reading is more complicated than following the designated basal sequence. High quality reading instruction requires quality instructional materials based on research and teachers highly skilled in how to teach reading.

Whole Language

In the quest to allow more teacher control and student choice, the whole language approach gained popularity. Whole language is the antithesis of the tightly controlled basal. Ken Goodman is considered the person most associated with this method of reading instruction. Goodman (1986) theorized that since language came naturally to children, so should learning to read. Goodman stated, "many school traditions seem to have hindered language development. In our zeal to make it easy, we've made it hard. How? Primarily by breaking whole (natural) language into bite-sized, but abstract little pieces" (p. 7). According to P. David Pearson (1989), the underpinning philosophy of the whole language is based on the idea that children are naturally curious and desire to create meaning from their experiences.

Reading, according to the whole language philosophy, is an intuitive process for children. Therefore, children should drive the reading process. A wide variety of reading material should be provided to students, so they can select the reading material that appeals most to them. In addition to reading, students should be encouraged to write daily about what they want to write about. The teacher's role is to support and respond to each of the student's interests (Goodman, 1986 and Sherman & Ramsey, 2006).

In the whole language method, phonics skills are taught incidentally or on an as-needed basis. If a child is reading and encounters an unknown word and can't figure it out through context, then the teacher provides the necessary instruction to help the student. Other elements of the whole language approach include invented spelling, flexible lesson plans, sustained silent reading, and a non-systematic instructional approach to teaching grammar (Sherman & Ramsey, 2006).

An essential component of whole language is a literature-rich classroom. Children need to be immersed in high-quality literature, both fiction and nonfiction. Classrooms filled with a plethora of books invite children to explore their interests and naturally nurture learning to read and write (Goodman, 1986).

Whole Language and Integrated Thematic Instruction

With the whole language approach came thematic instruction. Susan Kovalik's Integrated Thematic Instruction became popular. Teachers were encouraged to teach across the curriculum and ask broad questions that drove the instructional themes. Teachers worked together to develop and write curriculum to fit with the unit themes and grade-level expectations. Examples of themes are Building bridges: Connecting History, Culture, and Time, Immigration and Assimilation: What does it mean to be an American, The Environment: Love It or Lose it, are just some of the many thematic units teachers created (Kovalik, 1994). Even with a massive amount of teacher time and dedication to creating engaging materials for each of their units, students' reading abilities did not improve.

In the desire to promote a love of reading and allow teachers to co-create instruction with students in a student-centered learning approach, many educators became strong advocates for the whole language philosophy. However, students did not learn to read naturally. As reading scores tanked, Congress commissioned a national panel in 1997 through the National Institute of Child Health and Human Development (NICHD) to determine what were the best approaches to reading instruction according to the current research. The result was the Report of the National Reading Panel Teaching Children to Read: An Evidence-Based Assessment of the Scientific Research Literature on Reading and Its Implications for Reading Instruction (NICHD, 2000).

Defining Best Practices in Reading

The report of the national reading panel defined best practices based on the research which are still prevalent in reading instruction today. Reading instruction should include phonemic awareness, phonics, fluency, comprehension, and vocabulary (NICHD, 2000). Additionally, teacher preparation and teacher education in reading instruction are essential to teaching the necessary skills to children. The results of the report brought beginning steps in bringing research and educational practices being used in the classroom together.

Research in Practice

When schools and teachers implement best practices, 95% of students can be proficient readers. Achieving results where reading failure is prevented or significantly mitigated requires evidenced-based instruction beginning in kindergarten and building throughout a student's schooling by providing a solid phonemic awareness base, phonics, fluency, vocabulary, and comprehension all taught explicitly and systematically (Moats, 2020). Honing these reading skills involves having students read and write on a daily basis.

In the early grades, kindergarten through grade three is typically considered when students learn to read. Beginning in preschool and kindergarten, phonemic awareness develops a strong foundation for reading. Students learn how to manipulate sounds before having to deal with actual letters. Phonemic awareness instruction produces the best results when taught explicitly and in a cohesive and systematic manner. Once students have an understanding and ability of how to manipulate sounds, it is easier to link the sounds to the letters (Honig, 2001 and NICHD, 2000). With a solid foundation being laid, students are ready for phonics.

Phonics instruction typically begins in mid-kindergarten and goes through third grade. There is strong evidence that learning to read requires students to learn how to decode words. Additionally, spelling and writing work together with phonics instruction. While learning to read, students need to know how to encode sounds to spell words. Students need to apply their newly acquired skills to reading text and writing.

The selection of the connected text for beginning readers should not be too difficult. The level of difficulty needs to match closely with the student's skill level. Success begets success. If a student feels confident about their reading efforts, they are more likely to be motivated to read. However, if all they ever encounter is struggle, it reinforces feelings of failure or lack of ability. Reading material that is too challenging discourages them from wanting to read. By providing students with text that they can immediately apply the skills they have learned, students begin to build their confidence and proficiency as a reader (Kim & Snow, 2021).

Once students become proficient at decoding and recognizing words without having to sound out most of the words they encounter, fluency becomes more prominent in the reading picture. Beginning in first grade and continuing through fifth grade in most schools, student progress is measured through fluency benchmark measures. Students who read fluently comprehend what they are reading because they can focus on the content. Whereas when students read word by word in addition to sounding out words along the way the ability to comprehend is hindered (NICHD, 2000 and Honig, 2001).

Fluency or the lack of fluency can impact students not only through high school but into post-k-12 pursuits. Students who read fluently can read more books in a shorter period of time and in the process increase their vocabulary and scope of knowledge. Students who read 350 words per minute and read for an hour every day can read one and three-fourths books in a week. Compared to a slower reader reading 150 words in a minute who then only reads three-fourths of a book in a week. Over a year the good reader read eighty-four books compared to the slower reader who read thirty-six books (Jamestown, 1989). Over a lifetime that is a significant difference. Additionally, if students do not become fluent readers early on in elementary school, it becomes extremely difficult at the secondary level for the slower reader to bridge the gap and hope to read at the same rate as a good reader. Think of the impact reading rate has for high school, college, and work.

There is a moderate level of research evidence that supports educators providing connected text daily for students to read. Daily reading provides students continued practice with fluency, accuracy, and comprehension (NICHD, 2001). As part of reading instruction teachers can provide students with additional skills to help them become better readers and thinkers. Teaching students instructional strategies gives students the tools to improve their skills.

Teachers can teach and model effective comprehension strategies as well as how students can monitor their own reading accuracy. Once students have learned a strategy, they need to practice and be given feedback from the teacher. Without feedback and goal setting, and then refinement of their strategy usage based on the feedback, student improvement is less likely to occur (Deshler & Schumaker, 2006). More advanced strategies can continue to be taught through high school.

Effective reading instruction boils down to teacher knowledge and the teacher's skill of teaching. Do they possess not only critical content knowledge, but do they know how to teach the content effectively (Kim & Snow, 2021)? No program on its own can ensure students learn to read regardless of the teacher's skill level, nor can students learn how to read naturally no matter how motivated and curious. Reading is not an innate skill like language. It takes systematic and direct instruction provided by a highly trained teacher.

Educational practices with weak or no research base continue to be used by well-meaning teachers. Examples include how information is introduced and reviewed, teaching a new skill—like memory training—expecting it to benefit students in learning subsequent unrelated skills, believing students remember better if they discover new learning on their own, and if adults explicitly teach them new information students will not retain the information as well, and assuming students know how to learn (Truman & Altmiller, 2021). Additionally, using text with beginning readers that encourages using context and pictures to figure a word promotes guessing. As students move through school reading material no longer provides pictures to determine an unknown word, however poor reading habits developed in the early grades persist. It is far easier to begin with strong instructional methods versus having to unlearn poor reading habits.

In terms of reading instruction, research supports systematic and explicit instruction. However, some teachers not understanding how the English language works unknowingly perpetuate the myth that English is not very predictable. Actually, 86% of the words follow the letter-sound correspondence when being pronounced (50%) or consist of vowel teams (36%). The predictability level increases further when more complex rules are known. The percent of words that do not follow the rules is about five (Moats & Toman, 2009). Unfortunately, many teachers are not taught how the English language functions. Additionally, customarily used phonics programs in schools do not contain the keys to understanding (Treiman & Altmiller, 2021).

Instructional programs that teach letter sounds within words produce better outcomes than reading programs that do not. Good readers attend to each letter in a word as compared to poor readers who only look at some of the letters and rely heavily on context resulting in guessing. The good readers' process is so quick and automatic that it appears effortless.

Once students have the basics of letter-sound correspondence and how to blend letters into words, next is learning how pronunciation varies based on letter combinations and positions. Tools to teach children these rules are phoneme-graphem mapping (matching sounds to print), graphotactic patterns (arrangement of letters in words and the rules of letter usage), and morphology (units of meaning) and are part of the process of learning to be an effective reader, speller, and writer. Foundational to reading and writing is orthographic knowledge (Moats, 2020). When students possess knowledge of spelling rules and patterns and are proficient at using them it helps students remember and store words. The ability to immediately retrieve words results in automaticity. Automaticity allows students to read accurately and fluently.

Best practice for reading instruction includes a comprehensive literacy curriculum. Written language is more complex than spoken language (Treiman & Altmiller, 2021). Everyday vocabulary is more informal and shortcuts with grammar are often taken. Therefore, it is essential students receive instruction in vocabulary, sentence structure, and grammar. The purpose of having a handle on formal written language is to help students understand what they are reading. Not only does knowledge of formal language improve students' reading abilities; it improves their writing. Research supports that spelling instruction does assist students in becoming proficient readers (Treiman & Kessler, 2014). Further, teaching students word origins and strategies such as Word Mapping enhances their ability to figure out the meaning of new words (Harris, Schumaker, & Deshler, 2008). In addition to instruction in spelling, vocabulary, and grammar, instruction in writing not only improves students' understanding of what they are reading, it improves students' writing abilities.

Explicitly teaching text structures increases understanding and improves writing. For reading, when students notice how an author organizes information, they begin to recognize choices authors make in how to convey their message most effectively. In turn, knowing how writing works and seeing authors use various structures improves students' writing. Teaching text structures gives students a big idea of how writing works. When students are taught how the specific elements of a writing form such as explanatory or argumentation structures, they benefit from knowing the theme types. Students can then write on a wide variety of topics successfully by employing their text structure knowledge (Deshler & Schumaker, 2006). Writers become better readers, and readers become better writers (Cruz, 2019).

Structured Language and Literacy teaching encompass all major components of reading instruction and all layers of language. It develops students' ability to interpret and generate sound spellings, syllables, morphemes, phrases, sentences, paragraphs, and various genres of text. Ideally, a comprehensive program balances skill development with daily writing and reading that is purposeful and engaging. Reading and language instruction should occur within a rich, substantive, knowledge-building curriculum (Moats, 2020, P. 20).

Conclusion

In summary, a reading program reflecting best practices encompasses these elements: phonological awareness, phonemic awareness instruction, systematic and explicit instruction in the alphabetic principles (decoding and encoding), reading to build fluency, daily meaningful reading and writing, vocabulary instruction with word analysis, comprehension strategies, and reading and writing using different text structures (Moats, 2009, Moats, 2020, Honig 2001, and NICHD, 2000). Reading is a complex skill. In the real world, our new teacher from our movie scenario is just beginning the journey of being a steward of reading knowledge. Being an excellent teacher of reading, spelling, and writing is a lifetime learning process. Teachers who continue their growth in content knowledge and pedagogy will serve their students well.

Impact of COVID-19 on the Future of Reading

What is the status of reading after two years of a seemingly never-ending pandemic? Statistics from the US Department of Education (2021) report mixed results. Interestingly, some schools have seen reading scores improve. However, the majority of schools' reading scores have decreased.

As mentioned previously, education and literacy in US schools are not consistent. This trend of varying applications of reading instruction has continued and became amplified during the pandemic.

In the spring of 2020, many districts were not prepared for going to 100% online instruction. Teachers' technological skills were all over the board. Even if a teacher was technically savvy, the amount of work to transition in one whirl was overwhelming. The U.S. Department of Education Office for Civil Rights (2021) surveyed school districts about online instruction. During the first round of remote learning, students received less than four hours of instruction a day in 85% of the schools. About 17% of schools reported lessons consisted of previously taught material referred to as a "pandemic holding pattern." In the fall of 2020, 31% of the districts starting with online learning reported providing more than five hours of live instruction. Additionally, in-person learning increased significantly across the U.S. Despite efforts to get students back into school, the COVID-19 virus had other plans. As infections broke out across the Nation, students were plunged into further uncertainty. Grade levels, schools, and districts went into quarantine and were forced back into 100% online instruction. The back-and-forth pattern continued for individuals and groups throughout the school year.

Students across the United States historically, especially students of color and those with family incomes below the poverty line have experienced an inconsistency in the quality of education they receive. The pandemic added another stifling layer. It is no wonder reading scores are a mixed bag (US DE OCR, 2021). Ironically, some schools saw their literacy scores increase on state assessments. As mentioned, most schools experienced a decline.

Georgiou, Bacchiochi, & Soland (2021) conducted two studies on the impact of COVID-19 on children's reading. Their data revealed students in second and third grade, especially those students who were at risk for reading failure, were impacted more than other grade levels. Children in the lower grades are learning to read whereas students in the upper grades are reading to learn. Children in the early grades felt the impact greater most likely because they had not mastered beginning reading skills. Students in upper elementary and beyond who had mastered beginning reading skills retained those abilities. Granted, these are only two studies, but they could point the way for further research and in-house data analysis. Knowing where the greatest needs are for reading can aid educators in making informed decisions on how and where to target more resources.

School is more than a set of academic scores. Again, the pandemic put on view the multifaceted role schools and educators render to our youngest citizens. We nearly all have had those one or two teachers we remember. Most likely the first memory is your connection to them; the positive relationship the teacher created with you and the rest of the class. Next, you'll recall the fantastic learning that occurred during the year—lessons and skills you continue to use or build upon over the years. No matter the impact of COVID-19 the presence of these two qualities—relationships and teacher skill or the lack of their presence—surely played a significant role. I suspect students who weathered the pandemic kept engaged in school and learning because they loved their teacher(s). These students wanted to show up because of their teacher. Students who knew their teachers cared about them and their learning and would not want to disappoint the teacher by not showing up and not following through with learning.

However, for the students who failed to show up something was missing. A variety of reasons played into lack of participation. For a large swath of students, the system has let them down through a lack of resources. The pandemic shined a glaring light on these very issues. Students lacked access to the internet or a dependable internet connection (Harris, 2020). Additionally, the lack of equipment and space made learning impossible or nearly impossible. Some students were already hanging on by a thread of connection and meaning to school. The pandemic cut the thread, and they were gone.

Data on Impact of the Pandemic

The U.S. Department of Education Office for Civil Rights (2021) most recent data collection revealed two major impacts of the pandemic, a myriad of students suffering reduced academic progress and increased mental health and well-being issues. Additionally, the already existing racial and socioeconomic academic gaps have been markedly impacted negatively. The pandemic has further aggravated inequities in our systems.

Even though gains are made in graduation rates, NAEP scores, etc. the United States has room for growth in several areas that impact student achievement and lifelong outcomes. Data from the National Center of Education Statistics (2017, 2018) before the pandemic paint an already bleak picture.

· 22% of US citizens have minimal literacy skills or are functionally illiterate

· Fifty-six million adults ages sixteen to seventy-seven have low literacy skills meaning reading and understanding simple text is challenging

· Of the fifty-six million adults with low literacy skills 44% of them live in families with incomes below the poverty level

· Graduation rate within four years of beginning high school is around 86% – graduation rates have been trending down since 1976 (Baer, Kutner & Sabatini, 2009)

· Students from families considered being in the low-income bracket drop out at a higher percentage rate than students whose families are in the middle- and high-income brackets (McFarland, Cui, Rothburn & Holmes, 2018)

· Students of color drop out at higher rates than white students (McFarland, Cui, Rothburn & Holmes, 2018)

The Nation's Report Card (Irwin, et al., 2021) of data before the pandemic reported reading levels of:

· 35% of fourth graders performed at or above proficient

· 34% of the eighth graders performed at or above proficient

What will the impact of being out of school with adjusted schedules because of COVID-19 have on already bleak data? Will the data remain relatively the same or will it increase the number of students within the not proficient category? How would increased numbers of students leaving K-12 without sufficient literacy skills impact their adult lives? If students—future adults—fall within the lower levels of literacy competency what will be the impact on communities?

As educators, thinking through how we teach is critical. There is not one way to solve the current issues in education, but there is research to guide decision making. Knowing exactly the various reading and writing concerns first before determining how to address them is essential to success. An example that can be applied to educational issues beyond technology is something I learned in educational technology classes. One of the things that stuck with me the most in my technology classes was the idea of creating your lesson first then determining if and what technology would best be used to teach the content instead of choosing the technology first. Careful application of solutions, including the use of technology, is important in light of child development, specifically brain development.

When thinking about reading and writing instruction and the use of technology planning it needs to include an understanding of how children develop. Consideration must be made for what is best for their brain development, so the instruction will benefit them as learners. It is critical according to Wolfe (2018) that young children develop their reading brains with print first. Think about when parents read to babies or young children; most often they don't curl up with an electronic device. There is something very special about a physical book. With COVID-19 and the increasing use of technology, it is changing how we read and comprehend.

The use of technology for reading encourages or maybe invites the reader to scan and scroll quickly through the information without a great deal of thought. Due to this scrolling and scanning of information students do not develop reading stamina, or older students reduce the reading stamina they previously possessed. Recent data collected by the US Department of Education (2021) pre-pandemic and during the pandemic reinforce the sometimes negative impact technology and online learning have on children. Students do better academically and emotionally when they physically attend school. Engagement, attendance, and well-being all go up. Knowledge of these issues and conditions impacts how to best use the resources available to address current educational concerns.

While working with students in my practice, I have seen an increasing impatience with reading and comprehending details of the content. Students want to rush ahead and do the activity or just get the assignment completed. This is something called cognitive patience. Students are less patient with trying to understand complex texts. Further, student writing deteriorates. When I read how Wolfe (2018) described how our electronics impact our reading brain, it rang true of what my observations have been and even for me as a reader.

Wolfe (2018) explained that what we read, how we read, and why we read changes how we think. The influx of information continues to bombard us at a faster and faster pace affecting what we decide to read and how we read it. An over volume of information gives a reading environment of scrolling, scanning, skipping chunks of material, and moving onto something new. Often deep reflection and thinking about what we've read is not part of the process. More time on technology due to COVID-19 has compounded this situation. So, why is this so critical? The quality of reading impacts the quality of our thoughts. Reading with deep understanding requires attention. If you do not attend to what you are reading—comprehending—it impacts your memory. Without memory how do you build background knowledge? All these skills are an essential part of learning to read and reading to learn.

Parents and caregivers are seeing the impact of excessive technology and isolation in the form of meltdowns and other not-so-positive changes in children. The US Department of Education (2021) and the International Literacy Association (2020) report giving educators ways to deal with the fallout from the pandemic. Teachers, administrators, and support staff members are encouraged to practice self-care. Each educator needs to follow the directions of flight attendants to put on your oxygen mask before you assist others. Educators are no good to students and families if they are not in good physical and mental health. Additionally, if educators notice symptoms of burnout, they need to seek help. Information should be given to teachers on working with parents on how to help their children. Finally, the report provides recommendations to teachers on how to structure learning environments to support student learning that are essential to their achievement and well-being.

Dealing with COVID-19 and Literacy (Reading and Writing)

There are several suggestions I want to highlight concerning literacy. All of the guidance for support given by the US Department (2021) is contained within the Multi-tiered System of Supports and Positive Behavior Intervention Support (PBIS). My primary focus for literacy is captured in the Tier 1 supports:

- Intentionally connect with all students

- Use screening, diagnostic, and monitoring tools to plan
- Employ culturally relevant academic instruction
- Provide feedback that is specific and supportive
- Integrate social-emotional curriculum within the content

To streamline efforts to address academic skills and well-being, literacy instruction provides ample opportunities to integrate the two and implement the aforementioned suggestions.

Secondly, literature—fiction and nonfiction—can provide students a safe place to explore and deal with current life situations. As a young person, I found answers and examples to follow among the books I read. Books gave me comfort and solace. When encountering unfamiliar situations, I'd often think of how a particular character or person handled a similar circumstance. When I began teaching, I found my students could easily discuss issues confronting individuals in books that they would never deal with that they were experiencing. Solutions to problems came readily when helping a fictional character than when trying to problem-solve personal issues. Using the safe space of stories, students could process and find ways to cope with current concerns in their lives.

Students in my graduate classes have used literature in the same manner successfully with their students. Many schools read *Ivan the Great* and *Hatchet*. As an example, these stories deal with unexpected change, death, isolation, and survival to name just a few of the issues. As part of analyzing and discussing aspects of the book, students could apply lessons they've learned as part of the school's social-emotional learning curriculum to how the characters dealt with their challenges. What coping tools did the characters use in dealing with unexpected change, isolation, etc. Even discussing how characters made poor choices and what they could have done differently can help students. Reading and writing lend themselves to integrating social-emotional learning and literacy content. Also, it is a wonderful way to connect with students and students to teachers.

Throughout history, stories have played a vital role in humans' lives. Stories teach lessons and bind people together. Stories offer hope. Compelling stories provide rich and meaningful content to engage students and create purposeful reasons for writing.

COVID-19 has amped up the stakes. Reading instruction and getting it right are more important than ever. Positives I see coming out of the pandemic are increased technical skills and applications. Teachers have created a large treasure trove of content that I think can be used to support, enhance, and provide for flexibility in working with students. These additional resources are directly connected to the content standards. Teachers can use the content created with student instructional groups and free up time for them to work in small groups and one-on-one to provide students with a more customized learning experience. New and better content and pedagogical approaches can be a positive result from a trying and life-altering event.

Final Thoughts

Imagine what we want the future to look like for our children? Now is the time we must take action to create the future. Nothing will change without our conscious and thoughtful construction. The world is not becoming simpler and less complex. Today's students will be confronted with a world that I can barely imagine. However, as educators, we must prepare students to live in a highly diverse and complex world. They will face moral and ethical issues and maybe even issues on which the entire human race's existence depends.

Meaning, purpose, connection, and belonging are critical human needs. Our technological world has not decreased these needs. If anything, technology has increased an unspoken need for their presence. Electronic friends don't replace the close intimate face-to-face relationships humans long for. As part of a young person's growth and development, personal relationships are essential. I believe reading contributes to the essential components of what makes us human. Belonging to a caring community makes a significant difference. Whether reading instruction takes place face-to-face, online, or a combination of the two, positive caring relationships and highly skilled teachers must be front and center. Additionally, the infrastructure and resources must be in place to support our reading teachers and their students.

The main point I want to make is whatever the situation is that confronts us as educators, we must dig in, investigate, act, evaluate, and adjust. We can't let impossible circumstances stop us before we even start. Educators must believe we will come up with solutions. Imagine the possibilities, and then make them a reality. Work with others to make the impossible possible. Our courage, creativity, and boldness will inspire our students to become possibility thinkers. This will be a skill that will serve them well.

Chapter 4
The Impact on ELL Instruction

Carly Spina

Illustration by Isabella Giselle Rodríguez

Introduction

After serving for fifteen years in the multilingual education space, I can definitely tell you that our field is ever-growing, ever-evolving, as am I. The things I did, said, and believed when I first started in this field are different from my practices today. (And thank goodness!)

The term multilingual learner refers to students who have been identified as having another language in the home, and who also qualify for language support services. School districts have various ways that they provide these types of language services. Some offer English Learner programs, like a transitional program of instruction. Others offer bilingual programs of instruction that feature a language allocation plan that builds towards English proficiency. Still, other districts offer dual-language programs. Sometimes the program is one-way (all students share an additional heritage language other than English) or two-way (half the students share an additional heritage language, and half the students are monolingual) with a goal of bilingualism and biliteracy.

Terms change over time, and this demonstrates our collective growth as educators. Why is this important? Language changes based on context. Why shouldn't our practices also? When we are presented with new information, what do we do with it? This tells us a lot.

They say there's no greater optimism than that of a Chicago Bears fan. Growing up on the north side of Chicago, Sundays in the fall were devoted to gathering around the game and listening to my dad yell at the TV, sometimes in support and sometimes in frustration. To this day, Sundays in the fall are devoted to bringing my own two kids to sit with Papa and watch The Game. When The Bears do well, everyone celebrates. When they don't do well, we grumble and hope for a better game next week. We are hopelessly devoted, and yes - forever optimistic.

Growing up in Chicago, there were languages all around us. You could hear different languages in the music of the cars driving by. Houses of faith boasted signs that told parishioners what time services were in English and additional languages all across the city. Languages were present in restaurants, up and down the block, in stores and shops, and in and out of neighbors' houses. The linguistic diversity has always been rich - but it hasn't always been welcome.

The city of Chicago has an interesting history. The name itself is from the indigenous groups who often named places for their plant life. (Yes - Chicago means *stinky onion*!) As immigrants came from different places in the world and started to settle in the Chicagoland area, they would find spaces that spoke their similar language. This allowed communities to support each other in finding work, housing, and navigating a new life in a new place. There is still a strong presence in these neighborhoods to this day. All over the city, you will find different neighborhoods with different ties to cultural groups, as evidenced by their restaurants, shops, languages, houses of faith, and languages. Andersonville is popular with Swedish-Americans, Lincoln Square with German-Americans, Pilsen with Mexican-Americans, etc.

When my great-grandmother moved to Chicago from Hungary, she settled in an area of the city where there were other people from Hungary and Austria. She got a job in a factory creating fashionable hats. She, like other immigrants of her time, was encouraged to abandon their heritage languages and learn English. Because of this, no one else in my family can speak, listen, read, or write in Hungarian. It was a language gift that was not encouraged to be shared. Interestingly enough, the United States has no national language, but that didn't stop an English-only mentality to permeate through neighborhoods, towns, and cities across the country.

Fast forward several generations later, my family left the city and headed for the suburbs. After moving to the suburbs, we all felt a little disconnected. Nothing was within walking distance, and neighbors didn't come out of their homes very much. It felt a little isolating, even though we had language privilege, transportation, and could easily navigate around our new town. Attending high school in the suburbs made me realize how very different opportunities were just a short thirty-minute drive away.

I always knew I wanted to be a teacher, and I was able to practice and learn the Spanish language through privilege (by taking classes at the high school) and not through a need (to navigate and survive in a new place). I eventually graduated from college with a bachelor's degree in Education with an English as a Second Language (ESL) Endorsement and a minor in Spanish. As I entered my first few years of teaching, I found it interesting (and maddening) how I would often be praised for speaking in Spanish (again, a language that I learned out of privilege), while my students were never praised for speaking Spanish (their heritage language).

How Multilingual Education Has Been Traditionally Viewed

Over the years, I have watched how EL instruction has changed, right down to the vocabulary. When I first entered the field, we referred to students who were new to the English language as NEP - or Non-English Proficient. Students who were not new to the language but were still developing were labeled as LEP, or Limited English Proficient. Isn't that telling? The very first word we used to describe these students were deficit terms: *Non* and *Limited*. How degrading! Now, I feel much more comfortable with the term *Multilingual Learner*, which is the term that Illinois now uses to describe students who are acquiring English as an additional language. It is a term that honors all of their linguistic assets without centering English (like in the terms *ELL- English Language Learner* or *ESL- English as a Second Language,* which assumes English is a second language and not a third or fourth!). While everyone truly is a language learner (as we are all constantly learning more language), not everyone is a multilingual learner.

When I first started teaching, I felt like EL instruction felt separate from grade-level content. The support I provided was largely out-of-class support and in isolation from other peers. I rarely had the time or opportunity to collaborate with my grade-level classroom teachers, social workers, PE teachers, fine arts teachers, etc. When I was able to provide "in-class" support (via service delivery that is widely known as "push-in" support- *which is different from a co-teaching model*), I felt like I had to be quiet, pull kids off to the side (or worse- to the back of the classroom), and deliver support like I was invisible to the rest of the class.

I felt pressured as a new EL teacher to focus strictly on grammar, spelling, vocabulary, and isolated tasks and activities around reading, writing, speaking and listening. It felt separate and unrelated to what the students were doing in their classrooms with their classroom teacher and their monolingual peers. The overemphasis on language rules and conventions didn't make learning feel fun or come alive. I knew I had to pause so that I could reflect and improve my practice.

When I first began in this field, there was a lot of conversation about how "behind" our students were. I sat in meeting after meeting that described "gaps" in great detail. We would have meetings that would list out all the ways that my students "struggled." We used words like "low" and "at risk" to describe our multilingual learners. It felt degrading, discouraging, and disheartening. We never made lists of gifts, talents, assets, or passions that students had. Colleagues beyond my school district experienced similar situations, and many still do today.

As I started speaking with other EL educators across my state and beyond, I learned about how common it was for EL teachers to teach lessons in hallways or in "converted" closets because they weren't provided with an instructional space equal to that of their peers. I started to realize how commonplace it was for schools to be in noncompliance with civil rights laws, like not providing language access to families for key pieces of school information, such as registration paperwork. I realized how little effort was made to arrange for interpreters for parent-teacher conferences. The inequities have always been there, but I started to realize just how broken the system was for the students and families we serve.

As educators, we recognize that multilingual learners are not a homogenous group. The population is a huge umbrella term, encompassing various language levels in English and also heritage language proficiencies, experiences, and exposures. It also encompasses learners with various socioeconomic needs, access to resources, and citizenship statuses. It encompasses students who are gifted, students with disabilities, students with trauma, and students who are leaders in their schools and communities. (And of course, many students fall into several categories at once!) We also serve students with limited or interrupted education (SLIFE), students who are born in the US, and students who are new to the country and/or the English language. Reminding ourselves how diverse a student population is helps us to avoid making blanket statements about students we serve.

Defining the Best Practices of Multilingual Education

As the years rolled by, I had more opportunities to collaborate with content teachers across grade levels. I would stand side-by-side with teachers and deliver lessons *with* them. Later, when I was serving in an instructional coaching role, I was thrilled to provide support to a district-wide co-teaching framework that we launched in an effort to build capacity for educators in co-planning, co-instructing, co-assessing, and co-reflecting. This was a huge shift as it changed practices from individuals in specialized roles, like an EL teacher, from "pushing in" to classroom or content teacher's classrooms to co-teaching alongside them for the benefit of *serving all students better*, with particular students in mind. It transformed collaboration and learning inside classrooms across the district! "...Co-teaching team members have the power to influence how curriculum is presented to all students and to create opportunities for new ideas and strategies that can be undertaken with ELs in mind" (Honigsfeld & Dove, 2019)

Not all shifts have been easy or positive. We recognize that language exists in a sociopolitical context, and so it must stand that teaching language does, too. Anti-immigrant rhetoric has harmed our communities in many ways, including reigniting an English-only or English-centering rhetoric. As teachers, we cannot ignore the ways in which the political climate impacts our students and their families. A three-state ban on bilingual education (Proposition 203) in 2000 was evidence of many folks' desires to abandon the inclusion of heritage languages in schools in an effort to promote English proficiency.

As a field, we began to pay better attention to the language choices we used. As mentioned earlier, the terms even changed over time to represent a more holistic and asset-oriented term (*multilingual learner* vs. *non-English proficient*). We started to examine our language policies in schools and classrooms. Dual language programs (both one-way and two-way) have started to gain momentum across the country. Educators and leaders have been embracing the practice of translanguaging, which is a pedagogy that recognizes the full linguistic repertoire of students and encourages students to utilize all their linguistic resources to learn content and also make and create meaning: "Translanguaging... refers to the ways that bilinguals use their language repertoires, *from their own perspectives*, and not from the perspective of national or standard languages..." (García et al.).

We have learned more about the importance of designing lessons that combine both content and language learning, instead of seeing them as separate entities. Multilingual learners in our classrooms are being taught through language standards (such as WIDA'S ELD Standards) as well as content standards (such as CCSS or NGSS) simultaneously. Our instruction has become more strategic by embracing frameworks such as SIOP or GLAD across entire schools. We have begun to shift our belief that language learning is solely the role of the EL teacher, and instead, we recognize that language instruction is everyone's responsibility, since we all teach content *through* language!

In serving our families, we have begun the work of addressing our own biases and assumptions. Folks in schools (teachers, leaders, and every other adult in the school system) have started to recognize how problematic our thinking has been as we made declarations that professed that certain parents were "hard to reach," "not involved," or "didn't care." We realized that our schools were creating and maintaining barriers in terms of language access, transportation, and childcare.

How COVID-19 Impacted Multilingual Education

Shifts were beginning. Progress was being made. Still far from where we needed to be, we started to notice positive shifts in schools. And then March 14, 2020, found us closing our doors, freezing us in our tracks. We were left simultaneously panicking and also standing stock-still, scratching our heads and saying, "Now what?"

Teachers turned to their online communities for support, ideas, and resources. We started to connect with each other in different ways. We had to figure something out and fast. More sharing, more questions, more resources—and, as we soon realized and likely predicted, more inequities.

During our periods of remote instruction, there seemed to be an openness to co-plan, co-instruct, and co-assess with our grade-level classroom teachers and content teachers. Support was needed! Many of us were able to connect in meaningful ways with the teammates we served. We were able to collaborate in ways that we weren't able to before.

We collectively realized almost immediately how important communication with our families really was. For so long, many schools relied on one source of communication (a school or classroom newsletter in English only). Civil rights laws are there to ensure that families receive important school-related information from the school in their home or heritage language. How have we as a system been able to support this? In the weeks after the onset of the pandemic, schools started to pick up on the communication practices that our EL, Bilingual, and Dual Language teachers have employed for years. Recognizing that many families (including multilingual and monolingual families) don't regularly use email is one small piece.

We needed to share with colleagues that we can think outside the box when it comes to family communication. For me, I always had the best success when text messaging families instead of emailing them. Texting was even more successful than phone calls, although there were certainly times when I needed to make a phone call and have a full, continuous conversation. One mom shared with me that she cannot always take phone calls during work but that it was easier and more accessible for her to read a quick text message during her day. I met families where they were with their communication needs, styles, and preferences. When the pandemic hit, I was thankful to already have these lines of communication established.

Several families were wondering if they should remain in the US because of all the unknown. Some families wondered if they would be safer if they returned to their native countries with their support systems. Some families left without saying goodbye. There were so many uncertainties, and being in a new country with limited access to resources, friends, and family was too risky for some families.

School administrators and leaders started to take note of the limited access to technology and Wi-Fi. They also noted the importance of school breakfast and lunch once teachers started to share that many students rely on these meals each day and they experience food insecurity at home. Many multilingual educators (in EL, Bilingual, and Dual Language roles) have been advocating for these needs for years and we were often dismissed, overlooked, ignored, or brushed off. It was terrifying for all of us to think of our most vulnerable families being left alone or without our support. For some of us teachers, our leaders were finally ready to engage in these types of conversations.

We started to get strategic about the ways in which we partnered with our community organizations. Many multilingual educators already knew the importance of connecting families to needed resources such as food banks, clothing closets, social service agencies, youth organizations, etc. We started to become more vocal in our schools and on our teams about how we could serve better - because our teammates and leaders were ready to listen.

There was some initial panic about how to ensure that our online content was comprehensible. Were we embedding enough visuals, video, and audio to accompany e-mail messages or Google Docs? This led to great conversations about how to make all of our content more comprehensible to students of varying levels of language proficiency, and also other various accessibility needs!

Additionally, there was some initial panic about how many English students would "lose." While this did become a hot topic in online spaces, we also saw a reignited spark in heritage language usage in our homes! Families had more time to speak in their home languages. They shared stories, sang songs, prayed, watched television, listened to the radio - all in their home languages! This was perhaps a beautiful "silver lining" to the pandemic. This is a positive outcome that we want to continue to encourage. Our families should never feel pressured to "speak more English at home." Schools have no right to dictate the language choices of any child or family.

I can't paint a picture that this pandemic has been a positive change for students, families, educators, and administrators. It hasn't. However, what I do want to highlight is that the pandemic has given us ample opportunities to lead, connect, innovate, and reflect on how we currently serve, and how we can serve better.

Final Thoughts

Unfortunately, as we started the challenging transition of returning back to in-person learning, we have started to reignite some of the same old struggles that we've been battling for decades. The anxieties of "gaps" and "losses" have taken over much of our conversations about our instruction and our support for students. While these conversations rage on, it's so important for us to actively collect the language choices that we are making in schools, whether or not students are present. We must collect the language choices so that we can acknowledge them, confront them, and offer a mindset shift to ourselves and each other. When someone posts something online or shares something in a meeting, and the statement they made sounds similar to "our multilingual learners are at risk," we must acknowledge that there's some bias there. Let's instead shift the conversation and offer that our students are not inherently "at risk" because they are acquiring an additional language. In fact, we are the ones who are at risk in this situation. We, as schools, are *at risk* of not serving our multilingual learners not only adequately but with excellence! Establishing language norms before student data meetings can be a great opportunity for us to address the language choices that we've been collecting. It can help facilitate a conversation that is centered around assets rather than deficits. I always suggest that teacher leaders print out a few of the statements (with the deficit-based statement crossed out, and the asset-based statement directly underneath or next to the statement) on brightly colored paper. You might even laminate them or frame them to give them a sense of permanence! As your meeting facilitator introduces norms for collaboration, add on a few language norms to help guide the conversation. Here are some examples from the book *Moving Beyond for Multilingual Learners* (Spina, 2021) that you can utilize to get you started:

~~They're low in both languages.~~	They are developing in both languages.
~~They can't...~~	They can...
~~They're not motivated.~~	They're not motivated by...
~~They're low.~~	They're growing and need more support in...
~~They have limited English.~~	They're developing English skills.

It is important that we all continue to view our students through an asset-based lens and also a lens that is more holistic. The more that we can hold ourselves and each other accountable for our language choices, the stronger our schools will be!

Chapter 5
The Impact on Special Education

Dr. Tina Halliman

Illustration by Mason Halliman

Introduction

As a child, I knew that I was different from others and viewed the world differently. I seemed to constantly be in my own head and was perfectly happy there solving everyday life problems and navigating the world around me. One of my earliest memories of school was being in preschool, solving wooden puzzles all by myself, and more importantly being the teacher helper by passing out juice to my peers at snack time. The excitement and smiles on my classmates' faces as I came around to serve them were priceless! I am fortunate to still have my preschool teacher in my life as she visits my church regularly. She proudly tells anyone who will listen to the story that she knew that I was a very smart child because at playtime, I would sit in the corner by myself and put together all the puzzles she would give to me. Even back then, I was curious about how things worked and continuously was in deep thought. I carry this gift with me today of thinking about and exploring the way other people think and in particular the way that they learn. I never sought out to be an educator; in fact, I consider education to be my second career. However, early on in life, I knew that I loved to help others and received great satisfaction from serving. Hence, I sought out a career in the helping fields of psychology and social work. It's no wonder that I am a proud usher in my church and have been since I was six years old more than forty-five years ago. I love helping and serving; it is in my genes.

To know me, you must first understand the phenomenal family that I was fortunate to be born into over fifty years ago. My life in the educational world literally began when I was a mere fetus. Yes, that is correct; while my mother was pregnant with me, she began her forty-five-year-long tenure working in the elementary school district that she also attended and graduated from as an elementary student. Hence, I am no stranger to education. I guess you can say that I have grown up around educators my entire life, particularly, administrators. My mother was the first Black secretary (known today as Administrative Assistant) to work in this district and she worked her entire career serving and assisting school administrators. She started as a secretary for a school principal, then office support staff in the Business Office and she spent her last twenty years as the Administrative Assistant to the Superintendent. It is in all these roles while having her four daughters in tow that we observed and learned from my mother as she modeled exceptional work ethic, professionalism, networking, high standards, and achievement. Instead of playing house with dolls as children, my sisters and I would play, "Board Meeting," where we would emulate the Board President with the gavel (my favorite role), the angry parent advocating for their child, the teachers and administrators showcasing the great work in their respective schools, and different vendors making presentations. Little did we know that we were learning about systems, Robert Rules of Order, advocacy, speaking and presenting, and more importantly leading. It is no wonder that all four of my mother's children are in the field of education; two Superintendents, one Administrative Assistant to the Assistant Superintendent, and one third grade teacher. PHENOMENAL MOM!

Not only were my three sisters and I garnering leadership and service directly from my mother, but we also acquired skills that we learned from the administrators that she served. The first superintendent that she worked for we fondly called "Grandma Barb." Dr. Barbara Mackey was the first female superintendent in this district, and later served as an official mentor to me by being a member of my dissertation committee as I completed my doctorate in education from Loyola University Chicago. I stand on the shoulders of not only my mother, but all of the educators that she surrounded us with as we grew up. Every contact and experience prepared me for the rich educational career that I have been fortunate to have over the past twenty-five years; ten years as a special education teacher and fifteen years as an administrator. As fate would have it, when I became a superintendent in 2014, my mother served as my administrative assistant in her last year in the field. As a new superintendent, she provided support and guidance during my rookie year. Her knowledge and experience were invaluable in helping me to succeed. As a superintendent of a regular education school district and now the superintendent of a special education school district, my mission to serve and advocate remains the same. I firmly believe that all students can learn in their own ways. It is my duty and calling in life to champion this cause by advocating on a daily basis in all capacities such as financially, academically, and equitably for my students with special needs and inevitably all students.

History of Special Education in America

The history and evolution of special education in the United States can be largely attributed to key legislation, parent advocacy, organizational advocacy, and critical landmark court cases. The Constitution of the United States does not federally guarantee a public education for all students; instead in the Tenth Amendment to the U.S. Constitution, it implies this authority to the states. Education is considered the business of all states. As such, states individually began passing compulsory education laws beginning in 1840 with the state of Rhode Island. Compulsory attendance refers to state legislative mandates for children's attendance in public school with minimum and maximum ages to attend during certain times of the year.

Institutionalized to Seclusion

One would think that the enactment of compulsory education laws would mean "all" children including students with special needs mandated to attend public schools. However, this was not the case even after the last state, Mississippi, passed its compulsory education laws in 1918. Contrarily, students with special needs continued to be excluded by local school districts, and their decisions were upheld by state courts across the nation. In the case of **Watson v City of Cambridge** in1893, the Massachusetts Supreme Court upheld the expulsion of children the states considered being "weak in mind," "unable to take ordinary, decent, physical care of himself," and that was troublesome to other children. In another case in 1919, the Wisconsin Supreme Court ruled that a child could be excluded until fifth grade and sent to a day school for children who were deaf. The excluded child was not deaf but presented with a condition that caused him to contort his face and drool. His school claimed these actions nauseated teachers and other students. They also contended that the child required too much teacher time and negatively impacted school discipline and progress. Later in 1958, the Illinois Supreme Court ruled that the state's existing compulsory education did not require schools to provide public education to children who were "feeble-minded," or mentally deficient that were unable to benefit from a good education because of these conditions. Finally, ten years later in 1969, it became a crime in North Carolina for parents of children with disabilities who have been excluded, to force public schools to enroll their children (Weber, 1992).

Seclusion to "Perceived" Integration

While students with special needs were continuously being excluded during this time, the first brick to come down from a wall of exclusion to at least the perception of access to being included in general education came during the Civil Rights Movement. In *Brown v. Board of Education*, it was ruled that segregation based on race violated equal educational opportunity afforded to all in the Fourteenth Amendment. Essentially, this landmark case stated that all people, regardless of race, gender, or disability had a right to a public education. Specifically, Chief Justice Earl Warren stated, "In these days, it is doubtful that any child may reasonably be expected to succeed in life if he is denied the opportunity of an education. Such an opportunity, where the state has undertaken to provide it, is a right that must be made available to all on equal terms" (Brown v. Board of Education (1954), p. 493). And although this landmark case was a victory for students with special needs, we would see our nation now move the special education population from isolation in institutions and seclusion from general education to now being integrated into public schools but still subjected to segregation within these public schools.

Integration to Segregation in General Education Public Schools

The focus of Brown v. Board of Education was equal rights for people of color, but the decision was vital for students with disabilities as it propelled two cases on inclusion and access for students with special needs. In 1972, two key state cases were ruled on that charted a more defined course for students with special needs to be educated in regular education. The **Pennsylvania Association for Retarded Citizens v. Pennsylvania** ruled that, "all children with mental retardation between the ages of 6 and 21 must be provided a free public education and in programs that were most like the programs provided for non-disabled peers." Additionally, in **Mills v. Board of Education,** the District of

Columbia court ruled that the board provide all children with disabilities a publicly supported education and included procedural safeguards to ensure adequate due process rights. Parents played vital roles in the advocacy of their children with disabilities that had a positive impact on the outcome of these two cases and other cases eventually leading up to federal legislation. They started individually and in small groups to expand to create organizations of parents fervently advocating for the educational rights of their children. Some of these organizations include The National Association for Retarded Citizens, The Council for Exceptional Children, United Cerebral Palsy Associations, Inc., National Society for Autistic Children, and the Association for Children with Learning Disabilities. These efforts yielded positive rulings in several cases in different states across the nation, but they were sporadic and were not equal among states. Hence, developing and enforcing federal legislation became essential to adequately serve children with special needs.

Parent and Organizational Advocacy Leading to Federal Legislation

One of the first major federal legislative mandates that began the uniformity of access for special education across the nation was with the passing of the Elementary and Secondary Education Act of 1965. This legislation provided federal funding to improve specific categories of students which included students with disabilities. This Act had several amendments to it that added grants for programs for students with special needs and eventually changed the name of the amendment to the Education for the Handicapped Act in 1970. The final amendment to this Act came in 1974 (P.L 93-380 Education Amendments) that required states who received federal special education funding to establish a goal of providing educational opportunities to *all* children with disabilities including gifted children.

Children with disabilities were not only experiencing discrimination within the four walls of education but all persons with a disability were subjected to discrimination in other sectors of our society. Hence, another major federal mandate that significantly impacted the protection of persons with disabilities against discrimination came in 1973 with the passage of Section 504 of the Rehabilitation Act. The movement to include "all" people with disabilities became the politically correct language to use during these times. This was seen in the most significant federal legislation to be passed to improve access to a free and appropriate public education for students with special needs. The Education for All Handicapped Children Act of 1975(EAHCA), also known as P.L. 94-142, provided federal funding to states to assist them in educating students with disabilities and delineated the educational rights of students with disabilities. The Education for All Handicapped Children Act was signed by President Gerald Ford on November 29, 1975. We know it today as the Individuals with Disabilities Education Act (IDEA). Congress passed PL94-142 to mandate special education and services to children with disabilities in public schools and various public agencies which received federal funding. Children from birth to age twenty-one who presented with mental and physical disabilities were entitled to special education accommodated to meet their needs with fair and equal access.

Although this law guaranteed access, schools were failing across the nation on the degree of education which students with special needs were receiving. Hence, the courts were left once again to intervene and make a decision on what was considered "free and appropriate" public education in a student's "least restrictive environment" (Pulliam & Van Patten, 2006). This is where the landmark case of *Board of Education of Hendrick Hudson Central School District v. Rowley* provides clarity on the degree to which school districts are obligated to educate students with special needs. In a six to three vote, the Supreme Court sided with the school district and determined that IDEA did not require schools to provide services for disabled children that would maximize their potential in proportion to their general education peers. The court instead determined that IDEA merely guarantees disabled students a "basic floor of opportunity" by providing them access to public education. The court also stated that a school is considered to be following the requirements of IDEA if disabled students are receiving "some educational benefit" from school-based services.

This Supreme Court decision set a damaging precedent because it determined that IDEA only requires schools to offer services that provide disabled students with "some educational benefit," as opposed to requiring schools to provide services that would enable students to maximize their potential and receive the most effective education possible based on their needs. Hence, two key federal legislations were passed that primarily focused on accountability through researched-based methods that were driven to get positive results. The No Child Left Behind (NCLB) Act was signed into legislation in 2002 by President George Bush impacting all students in public schools. The NCLB Act comprehensively updated the Elementary and Secondary Education Act of 1965 by creating new standards and goals for our nation's public schools. This Act required increased participation in state-wide assessments by all students and highly qualified teachers for all students. If these conditions were not met, the Act delineated harsh corrective actions for school districts. The second key legislation that focused on accountability was the IDEA Amendment of 2004. The main topics addressed with the 2004 Amendment were to align the IDEA with the NCLB, to balance discipline provisions, to reduce the paperwork burden in special education, improve early intervention strategies through measures such as Response to Intervention (RtI) thereby reducing over-identification and misidentification, and an emphasis on transition/post-secondary services for students starting at age sixteen. The overall message of these two mandates was for students with disabilities to not only have access to a free and appropriate education but to now ensure results for students with special needs.

Federal Legislation that Significantly Impacted Special Education

Federal Legislation that Significantly Impacted Special Education		
Federal Legislation	Year	Major Tenants
Expansion of Teaching of Mentally Retarded Children Act	1958	Federal funding to train teachers of children with mental retardation.
National Defense Education Act	1958	Increased federal funding for the education of children in public schools.
Elementary and Secondary Education Act	1965	Funding to improve certain categories of students including students with disabilities.
Section 504 of the Rehabilitation Act	1973	A civil rights declaration of the handicapped helps protect persons with disabilities by prohibiting discrimination against a person with a disability by any agency receiving federal funding no matter if the handicap was physically or through a mental impairment.
P.L 93-380 Education Amendments	1974	Amendment to the Elementary and Secondary Act of 1965 states to receive federal special education funding to establish a goal of providing educational opportunities for ALL children with disabilities including children who were gifted.
Education for All Handicapped Children Act (EAHCA)	1975	Provided federal funding to states to assist them in educating students with disabilities and delineated the educational rights of students with disabilities: A. Nondiscriminatory testing, evaluation, and placement procedures B. Be educated in the least restrictive environment C. Procedural due process, including parent involvement D. A free education E. An appropriate education
The Handicapped Children's Protection Act	1986	An amendment to EAHCA providing reasonable attorneys' fees and costs to be awarded to parents if they prevail.

Individuals with Disabilities Education Act (IDEA)	1990	Amended the EAHCA by renaming it to IDEA to emphasize the person first, changing the terms handicapped student to child/student/individual with a disability. Added Autism and Traumatic Brain Injury as separate and distinct special education identification categories. Lastly, schools were mandated to create transition plans in a student's Individual Education Plan (IEP) by the age of sixteen.
IDEA Amendment	1997	The focus was on the educational achievement of students with disabilities. A. Including special education students in state and district-wide assessments B. IEP goals must accurately be measured and progress towards these goals reported C. Addressed behavior concerns such as ten-day maximum suspension and utilizing proactive measures such as positive behavior interventions
No Child Left Behind	2002	Updated the Elementary and Secondary Education Act of 1965 by creating new standards and goals. It required increased participation in state-wide assessments. Required highly qualified teachers. Implemented tough corrective actions for public schools.
IDEA Amendment	2004	Amended IDEA by mandating the following A. Aligning the IDEA with the NCLB B. Balance discipline provisions C. Reduce the paperwork burden in special education D. Improve early intervention strategies through measures such as Response to Intervention (RtI) thereby reducing over-identification and misidentification E. Emphasis on transition/post-secondary services for students starting at age sixteen

Best Practices in Special Education

Since the early 2000s, the primary aim in special education has been for students with special needs to make gains and succeed academically by utilizing researched-based programs. The major focus of many of the later federal legislation that passed impacting special education was to ensure that special education was held accountable for producing positive results for students with special needs. The mandated means to achieve this was the utilization of evidenced-based programs for these diversified learners.

Evidence-based practices (EBFs) are varied instructional approaches that have been proven to be effective through rigorous research leading to meaningful improvement in student outcomes. When implemented with design fidelity, EBPs have been shown to meaningfully improve the performance of students with disabilities (Cook, Tankersley, & Harjusola-Webb, 2008). When choosing an EBP, the instructional practice must be shown to be effective by multiple research studies that meet strict criteria related to research design, quality, and effect on student outcomes. When chosen wisely and implemented appropriately EBPs can be used as a guide to the practices most likely to work for students with disabilities (Cook, Tankersley, Cook, & Landrum, 2008).

There are key factors for teachers to consider when effectively implementing evidence-based practices in the classroom, keeping in mind that EBPs do not lessen the important role of an effective teacher. A ten-step implementation process for evidenced-based practices in education was modeled from the medical field where doctors followed a set of practices for choosing, appraising, implementing, and analyzing a treatment (Fineout-Overholt, Melnyk, & Schultz, 2005). The medical framework was tailored to education for assisting special educators in effectively integrating EBPs in instruction for diversified learners. Below is a proposed ten-step guide for successfully implementing evidence-based practices to achieve effective outcomes for students with special needs (Torres, Farley, & Cook, 2012):

1. Determine the student, environmental, and instructor characteristics (i.e. student age, grade level, need, teacher expertise, schedule, and resources needed)
2. Search sources of EBPs
3. Select an EBP
4. Identify essential components of the selected EBP (i.e. fidelity checklist or essential components of EBP)
5. Implement the EBP within a cycle of effective instruction (plan lesson, follow step-by-step instruction, have necessary materials, embed the EBP within your effective instruction)
6. Monitor implementation fidelity (self-assess implementation fidelity and request feedback and observation)
7. Progress monitor student outcomes
8. Adapt the practice if necessary (e.g. were all student outcomes increased with use of EBP, plan adaptations while maintaining integrity of essential outcomes)

9. Make instructional decisions based on progress-monitoring data (consistently collect data on students' progress, analyze data and evaluate effectiveness)
10. Become a leader and advocate and share with peers through multiple venues.

There are several other best practices that have been successful in effectively improving learning outcomes for students with disabilities. As mentioned earlier, one of those known proven best practices is *Response to Intervention* (RtI). Response to intervention is the "practice of providing high-quality instruction and interventions matched to the student need, monitoring progress frequently to make decisions about changes in instruction or goals, and applying child response data to important educational decisions" (NASDE, 2006). Successful special educators have also effectively implemented *differentiated instruction* to aide with positive student outcomes for diverse learners. Differentiated instruction calls for teachers to tailor their instruction to meet the needs of each individual student. In order to implement this best practice with fidelity, educators must use their professional observations of a student's learning and modify their instruction in the areas of the content to be learned, the process of how the content will be taught, and the product that the practice produces for the student by observing and evaluating their learning. Finally, the *development and ongoing monitoring of a students' individual education plan (IEP)* is essential for achieving positive student outcomes for students with disabilities. IEP teams should write measurable annual goals to meet the specific needs of diverse learners. Formative and summative results should be continually monitored to ensure results-oriented revisions to a student's IEP. Implementing these proven best practices in special education will ensure that students with special needs are making positive gains in student outcome learning.

Effective general and special educators all play a role in ensuring that diverse learners experience gains with academic progress. Hence, combining these effective best practices for special education with general high-leverage practices yields successful results for diverse learners. High-leverage practices include collaboration with professionals and families to increase student success. Using multiple sources of information to assess student's strengths and needs to effectively analyze instructional practices and make necessary adjustments to improve student outcomes. Establish consistent, organized and respectful learning environments to address social, emotional and behavioral needs of students. Finally, the systematic design of instruction that can be adapted to achieve specific learning goals should be closely implemented with fidelity. Examples of ways to design instruction include providing scaffolding support, using explicit instruction, using flexible grouping, using strategies to promote active student engagement, using assistive and instructional technologies, and providing consistent positive and constructive feedback to students.

The Impact of COVID-19 in Special Education

It is a fact that COVID-19 has had a devastating impact on our global world. The abrupt shutdown of our society, including institutions of learning, has produced undeniable trauma with many and in particular with students. The field of education is still learning and recovering from the devastating toll that this wretched virus has wreaked on interrupting and in some cases completely halting student learning. The overwhelming impact of COVID-19 has been experienced double fold for students in special education who already struggle to achieve and maintain learning gains experienced by their non-disabled peers. School districts were faced with multiple areas where COVID-19 caused negative impacts on the learning of students with special needs. One such area was in the need to provide 1:1 assistance through hands-on and face-to-face interactions for students who required it, in particular students with severe and profound disabilities. COVID-19 made it impossible to safely have educators provide in-person 1:1 service to students. Instead, once school districts were able to provide virtual learning, parents assumed the primary role of the 1:1 educator. Due to the inability to provide services mandated per a federal IEP document and the reluctance of the federal Office of Special Education Programs (OSEP) to modify or relax federal special education laws, school districts were faced with legally providing related services resulting in compensatory services for students who experienced regression during the absence of services.

In a survey widely cited by major media outlets, conducted in May 2020 with 1,594 parents contacted through Facebook by the advocacy group ParentsTogether, only 20% of respondents said their children were receiving the services called for by their IEP and 39% reported receiving no services at all. The pandemic has exacerbated the typical summer slide that students often experience during summer break and school districts are grappling with the effects of the COVID-19 slide due to the interruption of in-person education and services for students. This has resulted in widening the academic-achievement disparities for students with disabilities.

Another negative impact of the pandemic on students with special needs who in particular had specific emotional and behavioral needs, were the adverse impacts to their mental health and social emotional learning. By the summer 2020, evidence emerged from another larger-scale online survey of more than 80,000 secondary and upper elementary students that students with disabilities may have been facing more mental health challenges than their peers and more generally having fewer positive experiences with schoolwork than other students. School districts were faced with not only developing and providing social-emotional supports to students with special needs, but also being intentional with offering resources to parents and providing support and professional development in social-emotional learning and self-care to their staff. Some unique partnerships that districts formed to address these specific concerns were connecting with mental health organizations that were able to provide tele-therapy services to students and their families.

However, all was not lost in the field of K-12 with the spread of the deadly COVID-19 virus. There were surprisingly positive impacts and lessons that did occur in some instances that allowed students with special needs not only to maintain positive student outcomes but in some cases meet their IEP goals during the pandemic. One of the ways in which this was accomplished was through the use of assistive technology and instructional technology. Special education has utilized these services and accommodations for many years prior to the pandemic that made the transition to remote learning seamless. Assistive technology has been prevalent and even essential for some students with special needs, in particular for students with severe and profound needs who depend on these devices for their survival and educational learning. Hence, as result, one of the positive impacts of the pandemic was a population of special education students who did not experience regression but instead accomplished attainment of their goals and new skills. Although school shutdowns caused a burden on many families to serve in the role of parents and educators, this dynamic forced school districts to improve their communication and involvement with families to ensure that students with disabilities were receiving some level of continued education. Essentially, school districts across our nation had to learn to Pivot with Purpose to continue to cultivate growth mindsets not only for students but for parents and educators.

Final Thoughts

The impact of COVID-19 in the field of K-12 education has proven to have both negative effects but certainly positive lessons as well for continuing to effectively teach students. The ongoing evolution of this global virus has forced us to learn to coexist with it while ensuring positive student learning outcomes. Implementing many of the presented best instructional practices for teaching students with diverse learning needs will assist teachers with establishing and assuring positive student outcomes. It is essential for educators of students with special needs to utilize evidence-based practices, response to intervention practices, differentiated instruction, and high-leverage practices all while consistently developing, monitoring, and revising student IEP plans.

Specific guidance and resources for IEP teams to consider as we coexist with the surges of COVID-19 are to ensure that minimally annual IEP meetings are taking place virtually or through teleconference. IEP teams must adhere to the federal mandates of child find, eligibility, or reevaluation meetings for students per OSEP regulations. It is key to establish transparent procedures for parents to meet virtually. Consistent, realistic, and honest communication should be maintained with parents regarding the schools' ability to complete elements of the IEP while in virtual mode. Determine what services such as speech therapy, occupational therapy, physical therapy, etc. can be virtually provided with the assistance of the family while in remote standing or even consider individual meetings in-person on campus using COVID-19 personal protective equipment to ensure safety for clinicians and students. Finally, consistently and progressively monitoring students' IEP goals and regularly communicating this progress with families are imperative. One thing that is certain is that virtual learning/remote learning/e-learning is here to stay in K-12 education. It is up to us to leverage our resources to meet the specific needs of students in special education despite the venue in which academic and social-emotional learning takes place.

Chapter 6
The Role of Social-Emotional Learning for Teachers

Sara Bates

Illustration by Blair Bates

Introduction

P rofessionally speaking, I'm a statistic. I'm one of those teachers who left the classroom and left the profession entirely. I left my job teaching high school special education in the middle of my sixth year of teaching. Teaching was the only thing I ever wanted to do. I never considered other careers, and I didn't want to. Teaching always felt right to me. I would beg my teachers for scraps of classroom material and discarded books to take home during the summers to transform an extra bedroom in my childhood home into a classroom. For Christmas and birthdays, I would request teacher supplies and gift cards to the local teacher supply store so I could stock my pretend classroom. I would spend hours upon hours playing school.

When I became a teacher and had my very own classroom inside a real school with real students, I quickly learned that college hadn't prepared me for much of anything that I was dealing with—I was under-resourced and unprepared. I had no idea how to manage challenging behaviors and I struggled to learn to plan engaging lessons for learners with multiple needs, balance IEP requirements, and meet the social-emotional needs of my students. Though I was highly motivated to do my best to serve my students and remain in education, I struggled greatly without the support I needed. I made the difficult decision to leave the classroom to pursue interests in non-profit work. After having my daughter, I returned to work in higher education, working with students with disabilities and first-generation college students. Still, I found myself longing for the K-12 setting again and wondering if a role existed where I could combine my passions for non-profit work and advocacy with education and mental health.

The local community mental health agency, Bridgeway, was partnering with Lombard Middle School in central Illinois to bring a mental health therapist into the school setting to provide direct therapy services to students and families. Dr. Nick Sutton was the principal of Lombard Middle School at the time, and we talked at length about the position. Something felt right, so I decided to trust my gut and leave my position in higher education to become Lombard and Bridgeway's first school therapist. Honestly, what I loved most about the position and the program, in general, is that there was no real blueprint to do the work—we were essentially building a program as we were working it, becoming responsive to the needs of the school and the students. This partnership led me to my most satisfying and influential professional work.

Through my work as a school therapist, I fell in love with the intersection of mental health and education, particularly within the area of social-emotional learning. I loved designing systems and supports at Lombard that allowed us to create a culture of wellness and resiliency for both students and staff. A desire to serve in a leadership capacity led me to my new adventure in school district administration and eventually to my current position as the Director of Social-Emotional Learning and School Wellness for a Regional Office of Education. My role allows me to work with schools and districts to approach social-emotional learning and school culture and climate for a holistic and systemic perspective in the context of comprehensive school improvement. Today, I'm a licensed professional counselor, licensed teacher, and school administrator with a passion for improving schools through systemic change centered on school culture, climate, and social-emotional learning.

How Has SEL for Teachers Been Traditionally Viewed?

Even though social-emotional learning is what I live and breathe currently, I don't know that I had heard this term while I was in the classroom, and I don't know that my school or district had concerted and articulated plans for social-emotional learning outside of offering social work and counseling services. Even as a special education teacher, I saw myself as a content teacher. As I lesson planned, I focused on academics and academic learning. What I can say is that relationships have always been a focus in the classroom and as a new teacher, I was focused on meeting my students where they were and learning about them as people. We have to reach them before we teach them.

The Best Practices of SEL for Teachers

While we've considered social-emotional learning and the mental health of our students and staff in the past, the intersection of mental health and education still carries a considerable amount of stigma. Schools were unsure what their role should be in addressing the emotional and mental health of their students and staff and many schools and teachers believe that social skills should be taught and addressed at home. Mental health is often a mandated part of many health curriculums and many states do have social-emotional learning standards. But COVID-19 has forced us to examine the mental and emotional health of our students and staff more closely and respond to their needs, as we've learned that schools play a critical role in teaching social-emotional skills. Further, we've recognized that we must support the mental health of our teachers and that our school climate and culture are the pulses of our school buildings.

1. We must see SEL as an instructional practice. Student discipline, teacher language and behavior, and the creation and maintenance of safe, supportive learning environments contribute to social-emotional learning and development. We must begin to look holistically at student development and achievement beginning with our classroom practices. The Center on Great Teachers and Leaders has identified ten teaching practices that support positive learning environments, and can be applied to multiple contexts. These include: student-centered discipline, teacher language, responsibility and choice, warmth and support, cooperative learning, classroom discussions, self-reflection and self-assessment, balanced instruction, academic press and expectations, and competence building using modeling, feedback, and coaching.

2. We have to focus on teacher wellness first. We can't ask dysregulated adults to support dysregulated students. Teacher wellness and resiliency programs should be active and ongoing in school buildings and provide teachers with the continual support they need to cultivate and maintain wellness.

3. We must develop pathways for referral for mental health treatment and we must develop relationships with mental health providers in our community that allow them to become part of student decision-making and support. Schools should seek to create integrated systems of support with mental health providers.

4. As we develop and implement trauma-responsive systems, we must also ensure that these systems are equitable. Conversations about trauma, equity, and SEL should not be exclusive—they should be integrated and cohesive and part of comprehensive school improvement.

5. Allow healing to happen and recognize the need for a significant shift in the way we view education and the role of teachers, as well as the role of our students. We aren't the same people that left our school buildings in March 2020 and that is ok—but now we must respond to those changes and experiences, instead of trying to alter them.

How COVID-19 Has Impacted the Future of SEL for Teachers?

Among other things, COVID-19 is a mental health crisis. We've experienced isolation, grief, loss, anxiety and the list goes on. Each person's experience through the pandemic has been unique and their own, but we've all been impacted in some way. Our students were away from our schools and classrooms, learning through screens away from the routines and social structures that school provides. When our students and teachers returned to their classrooms following the pandemic, something was profoundly different. We have teachers and adults that have experienced significant trauma teaching students that have experienced significant trauma. Trauma changes our brains. We have adults with changed brains teaching students with changed brains. In this sense, we can't expect our schools to function the way they did before March 2020.

Overwhelmingly this year, I've heard from school administrators and teachers that don't know what to do to address the increase in dysregulated students and the social-emotional needs of both students and staff. Increased teacher shortages have left school staff members feeling tired, worn out, and without the manpower to provide adequate social-emotional support for their school community. Still, our educators remain committed to meeting the social-emotional needs of students and staff. This means placing an increased focus on social-emotional learning and examining how we structure and provide systemic social-emotional learning support to our school community.

Systemically supporting social-emotional learning includes thinking beyond a curriculum or how school structures support the social-emotional well-being of students and staff. This extends to family and community programming on trauma and mental health, as well as ongoing support for staff members that provide a continual level of wellness support. Schools should consider trauma-responsiveness in their discipline policies, emergency drill procedures, and assessment protocols. Trauma-responsiveness and social-emotional wellness should be foundational components as we rebuild and rethink education. This includes considering how we expand universal support for all students and how we create more targeted and intentional interventions for students with increased needs, including expanding pathways to mental health treatment.

Final Thoughts

"But I don't know how to teach about feelings and emotions." Maybe this is how you feel like as a teacher or administrator. And it's a valid feeling and ok to address. We have to address that—what makes you uncomfortable about social-emotional learning and its role in your classroom and school? We can't begin to really dig deep and address the needs of our students, school, and colleagues until we address this within ourselves. This means we have to recognize that just as social-emotional learning should be ongoing and reflective for our students, it should be ongoing and reflective for the adults in our buildings as well. Social-emotional learning should be continual, ongoing, and seen as part of everything we do in our school buildings. As educators, we can use our own experiences to teach valuable lessons and make connections with our students. In reality, your own journey, struggles and all, are the most valuable things we can teach and model for our students. Every interaction we have with students is a chance to build resiliency. Your morning was crummy? You spilled a cup of coffee on the way to work after coaxing your own reluctant child into school that morning? It happens—and it's ok to talk about—it's even ok to share how that experience may have impacted your emotions. We teach resilience when we share how we navigate our own experiences.

So it seems almost like a paradox to say that at the time we need relationships the most, relationships are the hardest to make and maintain. Creating and maintaining relationships with our students requires a significant investment along with a significant commitment from the educator to continue the relationship-building throughout the school year. Schools are places where students should be held, loved, appreciated, and supported. This is our emotional training ground—the place where we learn to interact with others, try new things and begin to shape our identity. And we can argue that this learning should take place at home, and to an extent, yes—we should continue to honor parents as a child's first and most valuable teachers—with the understanding that the goal of all learning is to generalize, practice, and continue to grow the skill.

A culture of resiliency and wellness is one that inspires that in others continually. This doesn't come from a single wellness event or professional development. This comes from a culture of care that is crafted and cultivated over time, as well as fed and nurtured. Social-emotional learning should provide the framework and blueprint for all school systems as we work to create support structures that generate healthy students, staff, families, and communities.

Chapter 7
The Role of Social-Emotional Learning for Districts
Jessica Donaldson

Illustrated by Katie Westfall

Introduction

I n early 2010 I found myself about a thousand miles from home, living in New York trying to start a life for myself. Up until that point I had supported myself with various counseling positions from inpatient hospitals to foster care to juvenile justice. After none of those positions really felt like the best fit for me, I found a job as a Program Coordinator for a 21st Century Community Learning Centers Program during the day while in the evenings I worked towards my master's degree. I was young and had no experience in program development, but my supervisor saw something in me and felt I would be the best fit to work with this population of students. My program focus was service learning, but the overall grant goal was to increase English and Math scores. I wasn't exactly sure how I was going to meet these goals since all I had ever known was counseling work and I hadn't ever actually worked inside a school other than pulling my therapy clients out of class when they failed to show up during their scheduled home visit appointment time.

I remember telling myself that if I just followed the service-learning model, I could make this work. It wasn't long before I realized that working with these students would involve so much more than just teaching them the importance of service learning. It was even bigger than helping them improve academically so they could remain on track to graduate with their peers. This job was about relationships. For some of my students, this program created the connection they needed to a trusted adult who would motivate them to show up for school every day. They were taught the importance of teamwork and how to create consensus for group projects and how to support the student who felt they didn't have a place in the group. There were tears shed and comfort from myself and the other students. There was so much laughter and sharing of new experiences. For some of these students, this program afforded them the opportunity to get to know their community as we visited college campuses for the first time, saw Broadway shows, learned etiquette dinner skills, and even explored New York City. A large portion of the students in my program were first-generation Americans. While they held very tightly to their Latino or Hispanic culture, they would often make comments alluding to the fact that they held themselves in higher regard than their classmates who were not born in this country or who had a harder time learning English. I remember setting aside my meeting agenda several times so we could talk about diversity and how the very stigma they impressed upon their peers was an experience their parents likely endured. Conversations around diversity, equality, and equity were happening for them in their enrichment program long before it would become mandated through the state. What I didn't know at the time was that hidden beneath the title of service learning, I was teaching social and emotional learning (SEL) skills as well.

A few years later, after I had returned to my home in rural Illinois. I was working in mental health overseeing crisis response teams as the need for mental health services continued to grow. Our small community struggled with very common barriers such as transportation, financial resources, and access to therapy services in a timely and efficient manner. Nick Sutton approached our organization wanting to create a partnership where we would house a therapist in his school. He felt his students needed direct access to mental health support. Remembering back to my experience in the schools in New York, I knew he was right. We collaborated and created our area's first school-based mental health therapy program.

As the program started to grow, it was becoming very clear that my impact was only as far as the counselors I hired and supervising them to manage the students on their caseloads. I couldn't help but feel that I could do more. I was becoming acutely aware that while I had counselors to support the students, no one was supporting the educators and administrators. After fifteen years of work in mental health and two educational programs developed, I decided it was time to challenge myself to do something different. I now support educators across the region and at times the state, by teaching them tools to increase their own mental health as well as that of the students in their classrooms. My vision has always been to create a happier and healthier community and I can live that vision by providing professional development and support to educators through social-emotional learning and mental health training.

How Social and Emotional Learning Has Traditionally Been Viewed

In the 1960s, James Comer started the Comer School Development Program to better understand how academic achievement and psychosocial development can be impacted by the environmental changes from school to home. The program utilized input from parents, school staff, and administration as well as mental health professionals to identify and address policies and procedures that contributed to behavior problems. Results within a couple of decades showed astounding improvements in behavior and attendance. Today, this model has been replicated in over one thousand schools and several countries. (Child Study Center)

A couple of decades later in the late 1980s, the W.T. Grant Foundation convened a group of professionals, led by Weissberg and Elias, to establish the W.T. Grant Consortium on the School-Based Promotion of Social Competence which set out to review programs that were working towards improving social and emotional issues and determine a unified framework for SEL work in schools. Their framework led to three categories of emotional: including identifying, labeling, expressing, and managing feelings, cognitive: understanding social cues, behavioral norms, self-awareness as well as problem-solving and behavioral: nonverbal and verbal cues. (Consortium on the School-Based Promotion of Social Competence, 1994)

The Collaborative to Advance Social and Emotional Learning (CASEL) entered the scene around 1994. This organization is universally recognized today as its work has helped to establish a commonly used definition for SEL and provided evidence-based research on how it can be implemented into the school system from preschool through high school. CASEL has determined five competencies for SEL including social awareness, self-awareness, self-management, responsible decision making, and relationship skills. (CASEL, 2021)

Districts across our country have implemented social and emotional learning in various ways. Curriculum Directors may establish a districtwide initiative to address the SEL skills of students by identifying a curriculum or program that can be used universally across the diverse needs of the district. Building administrators may converge meetings with their school improvement team to determine the needs of their school and then research the curriculum that is the best fit. In some districts, educators may be going at this alone, looking for lessons, a curriculum, anything to help improve scores and outcomes within a pre-packaged evidence-based box. SEL may have initially been introduced to some districts as another course alongside music or art. It is also not uncommon that SEL was offered as a group opportunity within the counselor or social worker's small corner of the building.

In schools where a multi-tiered system of support (MTSS) is used, some schools initially viewed SEL as a tier two or tier three support. Tier one supports remaining conversations around basic classroom rules - keeping your hands to yourself and accepting others and asking for help when needed - but for the students who were identified as needing more support, they were the ones that had access to the SEL curriculum materials. It wasn't until you were classified as having a specialized emotional or behavioral need that SEL was incorporated into your school day.

As the mental, emotional, and behavioral health needs of students increased it became clear that SEL should be moved to a tier one support where all students would have access. Still, despite the need being addressed, there were challenges with understanding how to fit this into an already well-planned school day. Suddenly teachers were expected to teach about emotions and behaviors. Educators who were already attempting to teach a great deal of content within minimally allotted instructional minutes were now expected to do even more with less time. The solution was to identify a curriculum with a scripted manual that quickly met the needs of SEL without the extra work of designing materials that would cater to the individualized needs of each classroom. Educators were offered a script they could work into their lesson plans and choose if they did it daily, weekly, or monthly.

The challenge with this view is that if SEL education is so scripted, it is difficult for it to align with the needs of an individual classroom. In the most recent years, schools have realized that SEL cannot be standalone support for students. It really needs to be pervasive throughout the entire school day. It needs to have the opportunity to be included in all classrooms, in all content areas, and in all environments.

Social and Emotional Learning Best Practices

As SEL has grown and developed over the last few decades, several SEL best practices have emerged.

1. SEL is just as important as academic instruction.

Many researchers have proven that using just a few minutes of class time to incorporate SEL practices can benefit educators with classroom instruction. Dr. Bruce Perry's research and teaching through the Neurosequential Model in Education discusses that the fundamental job of an educator is to change the brain. In order to access the part of the brain where we can learn, we must be able to soothe and regulate the lower parts of the brain (Perry, 2020). This occurs through regulation and relationships first. If our basic needs are not met, then we cannot focus on academics. So while the education system is focused on helping students to learn, if you do not prime their brains for learning with SEL practices, then you will certainly fail.

2. SEL should be embedded in your curriculum and school day.

SEL skills cannot be taught or practiced effectively in isolation. An article published by the Aspen Institute states, "it is time to move the nation beyond the debate as to whether schools should attend to students' social and emotional development, to how we can integrate social, emotional, and academic development into the mission and daily work of all schools. (Berman, 2018)" The authors go on to state that SEL should be for all students, starting with adults, and that strong leadership is paramount. All students should have access to SEL supports and skill-building opportunities regardless of academic, emotional, or behavioral history. Instruction should be woven into the lessons taught over the course of the day so students are aware that the skills can be used in different environments and settings.

As will be discussed later in the chapter, SEL can be difficult to teach effectively if it is not something you actively practice. Educators should be taught and encouraged to engage in their SEL practices so they can support students in understanding the benefits. To successfully create a district-wide SEL program, you must have leadership that supports and believes in the benefits of SEL. Leadership must encourage educators to incorporate SEL into their mission and vision for the district and their schools. They must not simply be informed of SEL practices occurring within their schools and districts but have an active seat at the table when planning for SEL materials and services.

3. There should be ongoing instruction and training for educators and administrators.

Just as academic content can evolve, so can SEL. It is important that professional development opportunities include options to increase SEL skills for educators and administrators to use personally or with their students. While the format of learning opportunities may differ within a district from workshops, conferences, coaching, consulting, or book studies it is important that educators feel they have the option to increase their understanding of SEL best practices and are provided with opportunities to utilize these skills. Social and Emotional Learning is not a destination, it is an ongoing practice. We must actively seek out ways to enhance our skills first and then find ways to adapt and support the needs of our students.

4. SEL should support equity.

SEL offers educators and students the ability to work effectively and productively with their peers with consideration for different perspectives and experiences (CASEL, 2021). Through SEL we can gain a better understanding of how our schools, families, and communities have impacted our behavior as well as how we can positively contribute to each of them in return. Instruction considers the needs of individual students and how they can best learn and thrive within the schools and communities.

How COVID-19 Has Impacted the Future of Social and Emotional Learning?

The pandemic has brought on a great deal of changes in the field of education. Some will lose their value once our new normal is established and others that we will undoubtedly carry with us for years to come. SEL's integration into schools was very much on the rise, however, the pandemic seems to have catapulted it into the spotlight and it is now a top priority. As schools scramble to determine how to address learning loss, what we cannot deny is that we all collectively have experienced trauma. Our social skills may be stunted, and our emotional and relational skills are now forced to look a little different. We are not the same so we cannot continue to operate the same. Just as we must make some adjustments to how we live our lives, we must adjust how we teach our students and educators. It is my belief that there are three components of a good SEL program that are paramount now more than ever.

1. Schools should prioritize adult SEL for the educator/administrator before it is implemented with the student.

There are several programs, authors, and narratives that discuss the importance of adult SEL, but it is commonly discussed as a suggestion as opposed to the priority. I have been in countless trainings and read many articles that use the cliche "put your oxygen mask on first," but there are rarely tangible tools and suggestions offered for how to do this. It is like telling educators to put their oxygen masks on without them having ever seen one or understanding how to make it fit for them personally.

I also commonly hear leaders say things like, "I want you to be well so you can be here for our students." This always gives me pause. What about focusing on educator wellness for the sake of educators being well? I imagine if we prioritized the care of our educators, we could decrease burnout and the rates of educators leaving the career. We must take care of our educators and to be clear, I don't mean providing donuts once a month or a package of pencils at the beginning of the school year. What I am proposing is taking something off their to-do list before you add some-thing else to it. Offering to cover their recess or lunch duty so they can have the extra ten to twenty minutes to just take care of their own needs. Understanding when they are well and not well and building in resources to support them. Offering professional learning opportunities that focus on their wellness or areas of growth that they find personally interesting. Leaders should also be mindful to not support being overworked and close to burnout with incentives and rewards. Instead, celebrate educators who have found a good balance between work and self-care. Encourage them to share their ideas and efforts with their peers. Incentivize self-care.

We know that anyone that enters the helping profession is completing a selfless task on a regular basis. We know that teachers are prioritizing their students and are always going to try to do what is in the students' best interest. Therefore, SEL leaders and district administrators should stop bypassing our frontline workers in favor of focusing on student needs and instead focus more on educator SEL and wellness.

2. If you teach, you teach SEL.

I often receive emails from schools with requests for professional development training to support their SEL Program. If the training is advertised as an optional SEL training, then those in the room voluntarily are the counselors, social workers, a few SEL invested educators, and occasionally an administrator. What seems to be the case is that if you are a classroom teacher, and your district is encouraging SEL, then you are provided with a curriculum and you stick to it. You focus the minimal amount of time allotted for professional learning on growing in your other content areas and allow the school or district to provide you with the SEL content. I find that many SEL curriculums are created almost as though they are a prescription. Provide this to students twice a week for forty-five minutes for six months. While I will not deny the benefits and at times importance of a well-structured SEL curriculum, the reality is that true SEL work should be individualized to the educator and student in need. We don't script self-care, we encourage it and let the individual determine what works for them. The same should be true of SEL. Can SEL fit neatly into your morning advisory time or your school counselor's lunch group? Sure. Is that the only place it should live to be effective? Absolutely not. SEL should be woven into every class, every day, every school year. It should be woven into sports team practices and meetings during extracurricular activities. If I am only teaching a student how to manage their emotions on Tuesdays in the counselor's office, then it is unrealistic to expect them to understand when their feelings get hurt on a Thursday morning in gym class that this is the moment when they should practice that skill they learned. We need to be teaching, reinforcing, and practicing on a regular basis if we want students to understand when to use the information in context. This leads me to my third point.

3. Mindfulness is an important component of teaching SEL.

I define mindfulness as learning to pay attention to the present moment on purpose without judgment. Through regular practice, one can learn to become more aware of their thoughts, feelings, and behaviors through mindfulness. If we can recognize how our body feels when we are angry, then when we feel those same sensations again, we will be able to identify that we are becoming angry. The better we become at this, the greater the pause we can create between what triggered us to become angry and how we respond to it. This pause is mindfulness. It allows us the time and choice of how we respond as opposed to immediately just becoming angry.

Unfortunately, I feel that a lot of our SEL programming is too focused on teaching how to manage anger instead of focusing on understanding when someone becomes angry. For this reason, I believe mindfulness is a very important component of teaching SEL. It teaches the "when" of all the SEL skills that often focus on teaching the "how." Elena Aguilar writes "Mindfulness is the antithesis of operating on autopilot, which is inherently flawed and even deeply biased. Finally, it guides us to align our actions with our aspirations and core beliefs, thus perhaps preventing us from acting on unchecked unconscious bias"(Aguilar, 2018).

Final Thoughts

As SEL continues to be implemented in more districts and schools across our country we must review our methods of instruction. SEL programs need to ensure all students have access to learning SEL skills and not only teach but encourage the modeling of good SEL skills from adults working in the school setting. Just as we learned from the Comer School Development Program, teaching SEL is not just restricted to the school environment, but it is also a community need and requires systemic implementation. Schools can also offer opportunities for parents to learn the same skills to use in the home environment while community stakeholders are informed of the importance of SEL to build a healthier community. Students would then be able to hear the same message and learn the same information as they cross environments from school, home, and community. While the COVID-19 pandemic has identified SEL lessons as an important component of curriculum instruction, SEL benefits everyone both inside and outside of the classroom.

Chapter 8
The Need for Relationships with Students

Dene Gainey

Illustration by Dene Gainey

Introduction

I t may sound cliche to say that "I've always known that I would be an educator." While I certainly considered various other avenues, I knew I wanted to teach since I was in first grade. There's much to be said for people around us who pour into us so that inspiration is drawn out of us. My first-grade teacher was more than content focused. She was character focused. She was relationship focused. She was so much more than a teacher. She inspired me to visit her classroom every year (several times a week) thereafter until graduation from high school. As soon as I was able to track volunteer hours, I did, amassing the second-highest number of volunteer hours in my graduating class. How does one inspire another to dedicate so many hours coming back to help? Moreover, why would someone do that? Suffice it to say, she knew this was bigger, she knew that others were watching, and she understood the value of being all-in. She was committed.

I am happy to say that I am an educator and lifelong learner in Orlando, FL with a Bachelor of Science in Elementary Education K-6 and Masters of Education in Instructional Technology. My masters was through an accelerated program while working full time in the classroom. I am currently in pursuit of a Doctorate of Education degree in organizational leadership. The majority of my teaching experience up to this point has been with upper-elementary students. I have spent the past few years in middle school, teaching English-Language Arts and drama. With more than fifteen years of classroom experience, I function in various capacities in the education world. I love everything about learning, including those off-content learning experiences. As I always say, "Lesson plans don't always go *as planned*." More to the point, some of those most transformative learning experiences have been those that didn't follow the original or traditional plan or format. So much more was gained, learned, experienced, and applied.

I've seen students thrive in a variety of ways when the classroom and the experiences therein are conducive to such a process. Like a plan requires cultivated ground in order to grow, so does the environment, both physically (the physical classroom) and mentally (being the whole of the student). My educational focuses or passions include: CLIMBE (cultivate, lead, inspire, motivate, build & empower), celebrating diversity, building community, project-based, and problem-based learning as well as the student-driven classroom. As an educator, it's important to build bridges and fill gaps, not to mention give meaning to learning experiences. My goal is to employ all of my skills and talents as a means to motivate students to be "more."

In April 2018, I published my first book via EduMatch Publishing, titled *Journey to the 'Y' in You*. Additionally, I collaborated on the EduSnap 2016 Best Practices in Education publication, on a chapter called "The Student-Driven Classroom." I am a contributing author for the_EduSnap 2017 edition with a chapter titled "Celebrating Diversity & Building Community." Also, I collaborated on Edumatch Snapshot in Education 2018, with a chapter titled "Ever Changing Nature and Needs."

A most recent piece of writing, published June 2020, includes a play titled *"Diversity: It's Not Just About You, It's About Us."* I have also written additional pieces of literature since then and continue to do so in various capacities. My "one word" to capture my goal and motivation as an educator is "IMPACT." Remembering these words as I enter the classroom on a daily basis helps me to guide my process. It reminds me that just because I have something in a lesson plan, doesn't mean that it is what students need that day, at that moment. Sometimes a deviation from what is normal or planned is absolutely necessary and having that sensitivity as well as awareness of the students you are teaching is vital.

How Has the Topic of Student Relationships Been Traditionally Viewed?

Relationships, or the idea of being relational, generally speaking, are not new at all. It might even be said that relationships are a human desire.

A country's history is an important factor that shapes and influences the concept as well as the practice of student-teacher relationships. According to Li (2016, p. 124), the student-teacher relationship is a part of education, and education is influenced by the society, culture, policy, and philosophy, and all aspects are influenced by the history of that region. How we view education today, specifically with regard to student-teacher relationships, is shaped by the past. French philosopher and writer Jean-Jacques Rousseau were responsible for the historical origins of student-teacher relationships. Carrying that forward was philosopher and educator John Dewey, who focused on child-centered learning and experiential learning experiences.

In Dewey's Progressive Theory, democracy is the aim of schooling. The curriculum is child-centered and is rooted in the ideas of continuity, or progressive connectivity as well as interaction in a social context. Learning is experiencing. We learn through experiences. Teachers and children decide together what experience is meaningful to each individual student's current learning needs and later development. Or, as an alternative view, students identify the path and steps that teachers should take to authenticate meaningful learning experiences for the students at the time. A learning experience is always a transaction taking place between the individual and the environment. The what and the how of student learning dictates, at least to some degree, the what and how of the student's future interactions (Dewey, 1997).

Curriculum and how that curriculum unfolds within an education setting should provide an enriching experience in the whole social context. Dewey saw teachers as leaders of social groups. Dewey further believed that teachers were guides, not dictators, and are responsible for helping students navigate and make sense of the world around them. In the same way, student relationships have been the glue that holds an inviting, productive, engaging classroom together. Naturally, students will learn more from teachers they feel or believe care about them. As the phrase goes, "Students don't care how much you know until they know how much you care."

Drawing Parallels

There is clearly no substitute for a classroom where the teacher knows his or her students and has taken the time to outline the students' traits, idiosyncrasies, likes, and dislikes in order to use them to engage students in a comprehensive learning experience. If a teacher knows a student prefers to approach a task or project in a unique, rather than a traditional way, understanding that student and having a relationship with that student, allows that student to pursue the task in a manner of their choosing, achieving the same mastery of content and standards. While the present-day limitations due to societal challenges have greatly influenced how education is carried out and policy decisions regarding education, the long-held values associated with freedom, interaction, and non-traditional approaches to learning are still vital practices.

Defining the Best Practices of Building Relationships

The how of student relationships may take on many approaches, all with a singular intent: to connect with students in meaningful and engaging ways so that the content being learned in the classroom is impactful, has value, is relevant, and ultimately is connected to the students in the classroom at the present time. Reading a novel with students in an ELA classroom setting may simply seem like something to do or a "task." However, if the approach to reading that novel includes thought-provoking questions, intentional connections to the daily life of students or you as a teacher, making content come off of the page, then reading is so much more. We now have relevance (making intentional connections, bringing students into the book), we have reinforcement (identifying why reading is purposeful and valuable to them), and finally, we have relationships (when we get to show that maybe the characters from reading have similar experiences as we do today, or even point out any differences or changes).

Intentional Engagement

While different levels of education require different methods of engagement for students and teachers, one practice seems to transcend every area: learning student names. Woodard (2019) also identified the purpose of intentionality. We all have different experiences, backgrounds, strengths, achievements, and stories. To quote myself here, "You are the only you that will ever be, your experiences, your story, your diversity." I find this to be a powerful statement because it identifies the strength of an individual. It speaks to the unique, authentic path of a person and how that aids in a complete picture, the full puzzle if you will. So being intentional means having that conversation about the basketball game last night, asking how long they've been playing, understanding their drive, and even motivation to pursue that sport. It means taking an interest in understanding their perspective or opinion about a topic based on their own set of experiences. Finding that "small" way to connect, according to Woodard (2019), leads to students' attaching value to the teacher and the classroom, reinforcing motivation and desire to engage in learning experiences. How much more does this sort of intentional conversation or dialogue with students provide opportunities to take what has been learned and connect it to the content being delivered? Woodard (2019) contends that classroom culture is enriched immensely, simply by carving out intentional time to engage with students in ways that may not be directly connected to the content.

Listening and Student Voice

It is agreed upon that listening to students is integral to building relationships with them (PBIS Rewards, 2021; Woodard, 2019). If we give students our ears, then we are allowing them space to use their voice. That is not to say that we don't all have voices, but again, it intentionally allows for freedom of expression of ideas, and genuinely listening provides you with the chance to understand someone else's view, perspective, or opinion.

A powerful application of this principle in the classroom is a daily quote of the day discussion. Each day of the week, students are challenged to consider the words of another person, which could be on a variety of topics. They could even be themed around a holiday, focus, or celebration. For example, during Black History Month, each quote of the day could be authored by a black American of the past or present. The quote is read aloud, students orally offer their thoughts about what the quote means, including applicability to life today. Modeling this kind of discussion and critical thinking is not only beneficial to encourage all students to participate, but it also allows them to see that it is okay to share your view, even if it is not the same as the person next to you. It helps students to learn how to respectfully disagree, but also add to the conversation as it grows broader or deeper.

Tenets for Student Relationship-Building

Education Trust (2021), a group of education policy experts, provides five tenets of relationship building with students: 1) express care, 2) challenge growth, 3) provide support, 4) share power, and 5) expand possibilities. These tenets are solid and provide attainable avenues for teachers to truly guide a classroom experience, which could ultimately mean taking a step back and allowing the students to drive the learning process. I'd like to provide parallels between these five tenets and the CLIMBE philosophy, which has guided my teaching and learning for the past ten years, gradually developed through teaching and learning experiences with unique groups of students.

- Expressing care includes making sure that students understand they have individual value, and all bring something to the table. The C in CLIMBE stands for cultivate.

- Challenging growth means that past experiences are reviewed and reflected on, but also that students are stretched to achieve greater than they thought possible. The I and M in CLIMBE respectively, stand for Inspire and Motivate.
- Providing support is similar to the pillars of a structure, holding it up, providing structure, and giving accountability for its purpose where needed. The B in CLIMBE represents "build."
- Sharing power, tenet four, identifies the gradual process of students moving from simply being a receiver of knowledge but becoming a sharer of knowledge and ultimately creating new knowledge. The B in CLIMBE, representing build, also factors into the idea of sharing power. Students ultimately should own their learning. It isn't learning for a class, or even for a day, but instead, true learning is something that should be cemented. It is that cementation process that leads to building new ideas, constructing thought processes, and creating the capacity to move from simply receivers of knowledge to facilitation of knowledge, creation of knowledge, and sharers of knowledge. As a cyclical process, the cycle continues and not necessarily in waiting to end the process before beginning again. That is to say, many ideas can be carried through the cycle at the same time and be in different stages of the cycle.
- Expanding possibilities requires opening of the mind to see what potentially is out there for students. Expanding students' horizons can help take the blinders or limits off so that they can see that the possibilities are endless. The E in CLIMBE represents empowerment.

How Has COVID-19 Impacted the Future of Building Relationships?

It has been said that adversity brings out the best in us; it shows us how strong, capable, and even how creative we really are. How do we view the present-day challenges in such a light that we can extract from them something good that can be used to propel us forward? I have witnessed a downward spiral in student motivation and even teacher motivation to some degree, given all that has transpired over the past couple of years. Suffice it to say, various factors have contributed to the feeling of so much more work or some much more pressure. In this way, it puts more emphasis on the value and necessity of student-teacher relationships.

It is easy to fall prey to the pressures of not meeting daily curricular expectations, or not accomplishing that which has been prescribed by a pacing guide or a lesson plan. Nevertheless, it is clear that a traditional curriculum may not be what is needed right now. Maybe recent events highlight the need to look at the curriculum notwithstanding and identify what needs to change. Perhaps there is a need to integrate varied types of learning experiences that are nontraditional. Also, perhaps that traditional assignment can be transformed into a more engaging and comprehensive project that accomplishes so much more than any one assignment alone.

Final Thoughts

Teacher relationships with students are non-negotiable when it comes to real, relevant, relational, responsive, and responsible learning experiences. Students thrive in environments where they feel that their teacher actually values their contributions and stories and seeks to connect them with learning experiences that tap into their own lives, perspectives, viewpoints, and overall understanding. We know that a classroom that reflects student-teacher relationships will be much more productive than a classroom that feels transactional, non-caring, and dictatorial. While those ideals may produce students who do as they are expected, I would argue that a class-room full of relationships will produce so much more.

Dewey and Rousseau's contributions to the education system as we know it, still have influence over what is important as teachers continue to work in the trenches to broaden the horizons of students. Curriculum is important, but how much more do recent events identify the need for something more than just curriculum? Our students need us in ways that they may have never needed us before. They need us to care, to foster rela-tionships that encourage them to care and to persevere. While many steps may help build relationships with students, staple practices include: 1) expressing care, 2) challenging growth, 3) providing support, 4) sharing power, and 5) expanding possibilities. We should choose intentional engagement, practice being good listeners and focus on the student voice. When we choose to be intentional about our interactions with students in the classroom, following these tenets, we open the door to the unknown. That is to say, the outcomes would be beyond our capacity to predict.

Chapter 9
The Role of Digital and Visual Literacy
Jennifer Leban

Illustration by Iggy Leban

Introduction

I worked as an educational assistant in college but began my official teaching career in 2002 as an art teacher. I had a passion for my subject, and I wanted to not only help students improve their technical art skills, but to make art less "scary," less pretentious. In 2005 I earned my master's degree in Teaching and Leadership. In 2010, I earned National Board Certification in Art (Early Adolescent - Young Adult).

I had been integrating tech into the art curriculum for years, so it seemed like a natural choice to go back to graduate school to earn my Technology Specialist endorsement. When our technology teacher retired, I took over the position at my school. That fall was also when my district first adopted a 1:1 Chromebook program, so I was tasked with writing an entirely new curriculum for sixth through eighth-grade technology classes.

One of the things that I enjoy about teaching technology is the ever-changing content. I thrive in a constant cycle of learning new things. I earned my Google Level One and Two badges independently and then decided to take the leap to apply to become a Google Certified Innovator. It's a lengthy process that involves creating a video as part of your application. Imagine my surprise when I received an acceptance email after my first attempt! In the summer of 2018, I traveled to LA, where I experienced what is probably the greatest PD experience of my professional career. I was surrounded by a group of thirty-plus other like-minded educators, driven by the same motivations as I was. We participated in a crash course on design thinking and were challenged to tackle our own issues in education using the design thinking process. Additionally, we were given support from coaches, mentors, and Googlers to help us reflect on and improve our craft.

As a result of these experiences, I have set a personal goal for myself to expand my leadership capacity. I obtained Google Certified Trainer status and started an in-district PD program to help staff earn their Google Level 1 certification. I have presented at state and national conferences, and have been invited to outside school districts to provide PD. I seek out new tools and technologies and use design thinking to innovate with these tools and make learning more relevant and exciting for students.

In the fall of 2019, I was named an IL State Teacher of the Year Finalist and given the opportunity to work with Teach Plus IL as a Teaching Policy Fellow. In the summer of 2020, I moved to the elementary level as a library/media/makerspace teacher. Shortly after, I was named a finalist for the Presidential Award for Excellence in Math and Science Teaching (PAEMST) for my work in computer science education. In the fall of 2021, I changed direction yet again and began working as an Instructional Technology Coach with the Learning Technology Center of IL.

In reflecting on my professional growth since I began teaching, the theme that has emerged for me is happiness and classroom culture. Positive classroom culture is closely associated with overall student success in school. With the attitudes and beliefs that I model for my students (through risk-taking and positive leadership) and reflective practice to keep curriculum current, relevant, and engaging, I know that I can help create a positive culture that leads to genuine happiness at school.

My philosophy of teaching focuses on three important elements that I want to encourage and support in my classroom: curiosity, creativity, and confidence. I believe that the goal of a teacher is to instill a love of learning and encourage the natural curiosity and wonder of our students and then help support students along their journey as learners. By adding choice, voice, and autonomy in our curriculum wherever we can, students will take ownership over their own learning and the content becomes more meaningful. I try to do this where I can, in student video production units, in personal website/digital portfolio curation and design, and even in small, everyday tech tasks, like teaching students how to navigate tech tools and effectively organize files.

My art educator background has instilled a lifelong appreciation and advocacy for creativity in education. Creativity means the ability to think big, to be novel, innovative, and willing to take a risk. Creativity means to try something new and different, to go against the flow, and not to be afraid to stand out or challenge the status quo. I taught visual art full-time for thirteen years before I moved to a technology role, and I still incorporate the brainstorming and workflow processes that we used in art in my classroom today. This is why the concepts of visual literacy and media literacy are so near and dear to my heart.

During the COVID-19 pandemic, I was profoundly affected by the misinformation and disinformation shared regarding the pandemic and its effects on education. My school staff, administration, school board, and community became a very divided ecosystem, ultimately resulting in my decision to take FMLA leave due to health concerns and safety. I've become increasingly interested in how technology, particularly in the age of COVID, has been and still is impacting ourselves and our children.

Traditional Views on Digital and Visual Literacy

In this chapter, I will present thoughts on why visual arts and communication classes should be a part of the core curriculum at all levels. I will advocate that classroom teachers incorporate art and visual communication concepts into their subject matter lessons. I will also provide justification for providing professional development related to art and design for all teachers.

MISCONCEPTION #1: Art and design are like whipped cream— they're nice to have, but "extra," and ultimately unnecessary.

Visuals are important for communication but are not always given proper attention and credit where it's due. My art teacher roots are important to my overall career as an educator because it helps provide a strong foundation (such as first-hand experiences) in how visual art programs have been erroneously perceived in education. Even now, most schools consider art class an elective, optional, or "special" class. When schools face program cuts, the arts are often one of the first things to go. I can personally attest to the fact that there are students who struggle in traditional courses yet thrive and find great success in elective hands-on courses, such as the arts. A school without the arts deprives students of valuable experiences, practices, and opportunities that help shape who they are and what they value. I believe that we should not only offer formal visual arts courses in school, but that visual design concepts should be embedded in the curriculum of every content area throughout a student's school experience.

When COVID-19 hit, I was teaching both art and technology classes. Both of these elective courses were made both asynchronous and optional. I honestly didn't care to fight it at the time, because we were all operating in survival mode, and no one needed any additional pressure and stressors if it could be helped. However, I still hosted a daily live video class session for students to come in, visit, and ask questions as needed. I had students pop in just to say hello, or even just to check to see if I was really there. I had students come in and ask questions about the assignments and activities I posted for class, but I also had a student pop in to ask me a question about his math homework! (Don't worry, we Googled it and taught ourselves how to solve it - woohoo!)

I also had a sixth-grade student that came into the meeting every day and stayed for almost the entire time. She would say hello to other students when they came in, and we would talk about school, and sometimes she would just mute her mic and work on other homework. But she was always there. Sometimes her friends would come into the video meeting and stay awhile with us, and other times she was perfectly content to be alone. I learned that even though my class was optional, I was still needed and served a purpose. Two years later, I received an email from that same student, just to check in and say hello, even though I had not worked in that school since I had her in class. That's a testament to how an elective class, like art, can support students, even when others may deem it unnecessary or extra.

Unfortunately, in the past, I've had students look me dead in the eye and tell me that their parents told them "not to worry [about completing work in class] because it's only art class..." *Insert eye-roll and a sarcastic thanks to parents for their support on that one! Talk about making your job more difficult than it needs to be.* Different students need different things. And for many students, that "thing" is art. Art is one of the content areas that crosses curricular lines and integrates a wide variety of skills, such as SEL (social-emotional learning), history, science, math, storytelling, and more. It gives students opportunities to solve authentic and relevant problems in a world where there is more than one "right" answer. Art gives students voice and choice, and the opportunity to be creative and collaborative. Art is hands-on, project-based, and naturally allows for revision, ongoing reflection, and remediation... you know, all those buzz words we love to use for best practices in education? Surprise! Art does that. Always has. Now, go find and tell your art teacher how much you appreciate them.

Although my response above gives examples that are specific to art classes/courses, art and design as everyday concepts exist outside of the art classroom. It should be understood that my argument extends beyond just the classroom and extends into our everyday lives and experience as humans in society.

MISCONCEPTION #2: Focusing on visuals and aesthetics in general is shallow. Caring about the way something looks is immature, unprofessional, weak, and feminine.

"Don't judge a book by its cover."
"It's what's on the inside that counts."

Although there is some truth to be found within these platitudes, they definitely do not accurately and completely reflect our human nature (in general) and societal practices. We want to equip our students to be successful adults, and in order to do that, we must be willing to acknowledge biases and psychological strategies that are used to compel us to make choices based on visual cues. We can harness this for good and help to protect our students from falling victim to unscrupulous practices. Visual elements can often give clues about the reliability of sources.

This is especially important when dealing with digital media, gaming, and devices. Does a website design look outdated and sketchy? Trust that instinct and dig a little deeper. Does a news article make you feel shocked and outraged? It's probably designed to be that way! Double-check that source before you share it out. Is that photo making you do a double-take? Try a reverse image search to see what you might find before you take it as fact. Visual cues, sometimes quite subtle, can signal "red flags" when determining the difference between fact and fiction.

An awareness of how visuals can be used to motivate and manipulate us is so important in developing informed consumers. For example, the color red immediately draws our attention. That's why notifications on our phones are red! By disabling your notifications on your phone, you can start to regain control over your time and attention (Center for Humane Technology, n.d.-c). If we fail to focus on visuals and aesthetics because it is "shallow," we are putting both ourselves and our students at greater risk of falling victim to scams, schemes, fake news, and phishing. Knowledge (and that includes the visual kind!) truly is power.

Visual literacy and digital literacy are closely intertwined. Navigating the web isn't a "fair" fight. We are susceptible to the algorithms and AI-recommended content that often sends us down a rabbit-hole of information, good or bad, true or false. It is important to equip and inform ourselves (and our students) to make educated decisions as much as possible. No one, no matter how educated or aware you are, is totally immune to the influence of misinformation. Focusing on visuals can be a key strategy for identifying and fighting back against misinformation.

Let's switch gears for a moment and think about how branding/visuals are used as a strategy in business. It is fairly common to find adults who balk at the concept of being an "influencer" as a potential career path, but many of these influencers, including esports athletes, YouTubers, etc are making big money. A determining factor to their success is often the aesthetics of their brand. Is it cohesive? Is it clear and easy to identify? Is it appealing? Being visually literate is a key component to finding success in these fields.

In fact, if you haven't thought about your branding, it's honestly not a bad idea to start doing so. It can help you get a job, make you more memorable, and assist you in telling your story. Like it or not, first impressions are important. To even further my use of cliches in this chapter, it's like "dressing for the job you want," and not necessarily, "the job that you have." Students and teachers alike can benefit from an awareness and understanding of how visuals can be used as a tool for promotion across any career path.

Think to yourself for a moment... Why do we make the choices that we do? When you're out shopping, what draws you to one product over another? Apple's design aesthetics are gorgeous. Part of what keeps people loyal to the brand is the design and simplicity. Heck, I own a purple iPhone and a purple iMac - they make me so happy when I look at them, and we can all use a little extra happiness anywhere we can find it right now. Why do we remember some commercials, but not others? Why do we choose to follow some people and profiles over others on social media? It's probably due to a whole lot of visual elements, so let's harness this power for good.

Is caring about visuals shallow and/or unprofessional? Or can both be true: that you can appreciate "fun" visuals and good design AND be a respected professional? Let's dig a little deeper. I am an adult that uses emojis and GIFs regularly as a mode of communication. If you text me, it's pretty likely that I'll reply using one of those mediums. Unfortunately, a person who engages in these types of behaviors (and other related forms of caring about/use of visual design) is sadly often viewed as immature and/or unprofessional. I'm sorry, but I REALLY care about design elements, like fonts and colors. If I'm a teacher sitting in a PD session and the aspect ratio on a photo in the presentation has been squished, or the fonts are mismatched, I'm going to have a hard time hearing the message – not because I'm judging the presenter (well, maybe just a little) – but because I'm absolutely fixated on that inconsistency, and it has sucked my attention away like Doug the dog from the movie *Up*. "…Squirrel!" They've lost me.

And you know what? It's likely that there are students in your class like me and you might be losing them, too, for similar reasons. So yes, it's important to pay attention to design and formatting and how your lessons look, even if you do it initially in the name of differentiating for students like me. Good design and clear visual communication is an element of UDL, or Universal Design for Learning. Universal Design for Learning is a framework to make learning accessible for all learners based on scientific insights into how people learn best (CAST, 2022). Good visual design can support students across language barriers and reading proficiency levels. By using visuals to help enhance and simplify communication, we can make our teaching clearer and more effective. What is initially viewed as an accommodation or modification for one group can ultimately benefit the entire population.

The way you set up your classroom (both digital and physical, for all teachers of all subjects and grade levels) can have a positive impact on student engagement, culture, and motivation. When you walk into a classroom, you look around. You make decisions, whether they are conscious or unconscious, based on how it looks. Is this an exciting class or a boring class? Is it happy or sad? Does it look like we need to sit in assigned seats in rows all day, or does it look like we get to move around and be comfortable and choose a variety of working and seating options? Does this classroom look safe and inviting, or do I feel uncomfortable and like I don't belong? Do I see myself reflected in the curriculum and design?

Would you rather learn in a room with bare cork boards, or one with a colorful backdrop and student work examples proudly posted? Now, we have all seen stereotypical "Pinterest" classrooms and rolled our eyes, and we should NOT be spending our own personal money to make our classrooms "prettier." However, visual appeal (and the amount of care and attention we put into it) isn't something to be completely ignored or shunned because of these intimidating examples of what we see online. Visual design is a spectrum. Too little or too much - neither is a good thing. Like most things in life, finding a balance is key, and what that means will be different for each person. The way you care for your space is, in a way, a visual representation of yourself as an educator, and your students will pick up on that.

In case it wasn't super clear, I do strongly believe that both can be true: that you can have fun and be playful AND be a respected professional with knowledge and experience to share, and that some administrators (and other education professionals) need to shake off many of these long-held stereotypes. Here are a couple of examples.

Kim Thomas, a friend of mine and 2016 Illinois State Teacher of the Year (Thomas, n.d.), shared a story with me about a conference event where she was presenting. When the organizers of the conference read her session description, they wanted her to change it because they claimed it wasn't "professional" enough. Kim is an amazing, passionate, enthusiastic math teacher who walks to the beat of her own drum - she mashes up words to infuse math terms into her vocabulary, and numbers are never stated in a straightforward manner. If today is the thirteenth of the month, Kim will tell you it's the "5x2+3" of the month. A conversation with her keeps my math skills sharp! She sings and dances and doesn't care what others think. But these attributes are what makes Kim, KIM. She teaches at an alternative school, and her classes are memorable and exciting. She has a unique bond with her students, who have struggled in traditional education settings. Asking Kim to adhere to traditional stereotypical "professional" standards would suck the life out of her, and erases all of the magic that is Kim. At this conference event, she refused to strip down her presentation, and as a result, ended up having a completely packed room for her session!

Similarly, I was once criticized for using the phrase "Oh snap!" during an interview once when I got too excited about what I was saying. I was labeled too "informal." I, too, was falling victim to the stereotypical "professional" standards trope. I've proved myself as a good educator over and over again, yet I still get labeled by those who don't know any better. We really need to shift our thinking on this one. Just like our students shouldn't be put into cookie-cutter molds, our educators should be given the same freedom to honor our true selves without being lumped into categories and labels.

The Best Practices of Digital Literacy
Graphic Design + Visual Communication

Visual/Media Literacy instruction is an important critical thinking skill. Specific instruction in consuming and creating visual communication is an important skill for our learners. Earlier in the chapter, I touched on how we can be manipulated through images and design elements, unconsciously drawing our attention and sparking emotion to take action.

UX (User Experience) and UI (User Interface) design is a career field devoted to how we interact with technology based on design and usability. UI focuses primarily on how the user interacts with the technology itself (functionality - how does it work?), and UX focuses on the user's experience when interacting with the technology and has a more empathy-based approach due to its user-centered design (Adobe, 2021). UX therefore, is more intertwined with social-emotional elements, and is something that teachers should always consider in their curriculum by asking themselves questions like, "If I was a student in my class, seeing this assignment for the very first time, would it be clear to me what I needed to do and how to do it?"

One strategy to assist in improving lesson design is to sit down as a team, department, or even individually... look at your lessons, and decide if there are steps that you can take to improve and help clarify existing curricular materials. Is there a color that you can use to help highlight essential concepts, vocabulary, or directions? Are there images or icons to help struggling readers find specific sections of a text or assignment? Are there confusing or unnecessary elements that can be taken out to help clarify the concept?

Another way to support instruction is to build relationships with your students and to be informed on what they're interested in. It helps to keep the content relevant and allows you to make real-world connections to student life outside of school. One example is through the use of memes and GIFs. Memes and GIFs can be powerful visual tools for teaching and learning (Reyes, 2018). By utilizing some of the same visual language that your students are, you have an opportunity to represent curricular concepts in alternative ways outside that of a textbook or lecture, which gives your students additional pathways to understanding.

Visual Storytelling/Multimedia Video

Common Core ELA standards include skills rooted in visual communication concepts and require students to be able to "read" visual images in addition to traditional language skills. Learners must be able to incorporate visual information and evaluate various media and formats (Common Core State Standards Initiative, n.d.). Image analysis in the classroom is one way to instruct students on how to "read" images in a variety of curricular areas (Finley, 2014). With image analysis, students practice a strategy where they observe, interpret, and evaluate what they see while looking at a photo, cartoon, video, map, poster, or other visual element (Finley, 2014). But learning how to "read" and consume visuals is only one half of the equation. Students need to find proficiency in being both consumers and creators.

The power of combining quantitative with qualitative data allows students to tell more powerful, impactful stories that leave a lasting impression. It has been found that students can better learn to decipher, understand, and communicate with images by developing their own ability to create images (Tillmann, 2012). Allowing opportunities for students to infuse personal expression and storytelling in the curriculum is a good way to practice this skill. Integrating video and multimedia tools is an engaging way to allow students to demonstrate understanding and mastery of concepts across a variety of subject areas.

In addition, being able to step back as a creator and look at your work as a consumer is critically important to being successful. The Institute of Museum and Library Services has listed Visual Literacy as one of their essential 21st Century Skills, alongside Information Literacy, Media Literacy, and ICT (Information, Communications, and Technology) Literacy (Institute of Museum and Library Services, n.d.).

Sketchnoting

Educational research has shown that visuals promote a greater degree of learning. In her research, Suzanne Stokes defines visual literacy as the ability to interpret and generate images for communicating ideas and concepts. Stokes reviewed studies that investigated the effects of instruction with varying degrees of visual aids, including no visual aids, still visual aids, and animated visual sequences. Stokes wanted to raise awareness of using visual enhancements in instruction and to promote the development of learners' visual skills in conjunction with verbal, reading, and mathematical skills (Stokes, 2002).

Sketchnoting is an excellent way to incorporate visual representations to promote a deeper understanding of curricular content into our current teaching practices. Incorporating visuals can also help support individuals with disabilities (Kluth, 2017). Visual representation helps with information processing and retention, so it's a good idea to encourage students to represent concepts in visual form in conjunction with words. Have you ever tried out Pear Deck Flashcard Factory (Pear Deck, n.d.)? It utilizes this concept very well! With Flashcard Factory, students can learn vocabulary in an engaging way. Students work together to create interactive flashcards. By illustrating and defining terms, students make learning vocab an active and social activity!

Drawing and sketchnoting can have excellent SEL benefits in addition to helping students gain deeper understanding and retention of curricular concepts. Sketchnoting encourages mindfulness and focus on a single task, which encourages calmness. Sketchnoting can be incorporated into every subject area, and one does not need to be "artistic" to do it! Sketchnoting can also be used as a strategy for mixing up your teaching strategies, thus keeping students engaged and interested. For easy, simple ways to begin incorporating sketchnoting into your class, start by drawing icons - what are key symbols, objects, or vocabulary for your content? How can objects be used to represent abstract ideas? Sylvia Duckworth has an extensive collection of icons and ideas for sketchnoting in her book, *How to Sketchnote: A Step-by-Step Manual for Teachers and Students* (Duckworth, 2018).

From a teaching perspective, one of the best parts of sketchnoting is that it is so easy to do. All you need is a writing tool and some scrap paper. Sure, you can get fancier, or take it digital, but at its core, sketchnoting is just doodling with a purpose. It's the single most simple way to add visuals into your instruction, and by empowering students to be the creators, you deepen understanding and connection to the content.

How COVID-19 Has Impacted the Future of Digital Literacy?

Visual communication is more important now than ever, and COVID-19 helped prove this point. COVID-19 has impacted our motivation and caused burnout beyond what many of us ever imagined. From a teacher standpoint, many educators expressed exhaustion and frustration over teaching a grid of "black boxes" when students chose to turn cameras off during virtual instruction. The importance of using visual cues and digital organization/simplicity is heightened. From a student standpoint, staring at a screen all day is rough. Too much of any one type of instruction (reading text, watching a lecture) will quickly lead to burnout and disengagement. Students struggle to have the self-discipline to stay focused when so many other, often more appealing, distractions tug at their attention simultaneously.

In my personal experience, working with pre- and early readers remotely throughout the pandemic has emphasized the need for a variety of visual strategies in instruction: a simple, easy to navigate user experience, combined with visual cues and design elements (such as color coding) are key in communication with students. Even proficient readers and older students can benefit from these strategies. UDL strikes again!

When I moved from junior high to elementary, I quickly learned that there were additional visual considerations than I had been previously aware of when designing curriculum. Students in kindergarten and first grade can't really read! And when they do start reading, they definitely cannot read cursive and script fonts, so stay away from all of those. Have you ever really looked at fonts closely and thought about how an early reader might see it? Until I taught that level, I had not! Let's look at the lowercase letter "a," for example. A standard font like Times New Roman would be really confusing. The letter "a" looks nothing like the one our littles are learning how to read and write! It has an extra curvy line up at the top that they've never seen before. You know what else looks weird to them? The letter "g." It's got a loop on the bottom instead of the "hook" they're learning to form when writing.

Visual communication concepts, when utilized in conjunction with Universal Design for Learning Guidelines, can help promote equity and make curriculum more accessible. This includes providing options for perception, providing options for language and symbols, and providing options for comprehension (CAST, 2018). Knowing how to use basic elements of art and design is a valuable skill that all educators can benefit from as professionals. Perhaps basic design/graphic design should be a part of pre-service teacher training? (Tillmann, 2012)

Visual and Digital Literacy (Information Literacy)

Visual literacy and digital literacy go hand-in-hand. As I touched on briefly earlier in this chapter, a basic visual scan of a website or news story will provide clues as to whether or not information contained within is reliable. A wonky, outdated design is a sure-fire signal to a viewer that a website may not be reputable. Sensational images and design (flashing text or animations to draw attention to specific links to click) should definitely draw skepticism. But as time goes on, technology is growing smarter and smarter, and spotting misinformation and disinformation becomes more and more difficult. Because of this, it is important for us to look beyond the obvious and dig deeper to try our best to make good choices and stay informed via reputable, reliable sources.

Think about advertising—how do we know if a website is reputable and not a scam? Ads you see on Instagram are often sketchy on reliability and/or sell overpriced goods, yet you are often bombarded with these ads over and over until they seem attractive and popular. Many consumers don't have an awareness of the asymmetrical relationship between humans and AI algorithms that recommend targeted ads to us. Persuasive technology is being used for good and bad. If we are not cautious and aware (and do not in turn teach our students how to be cautious and aware!) our social media feeds can quickly become echo chambers to whatever misinformation has persuaded us to believe.

If you have not yet watched *The Social Dilemma*, I highly recommend it, as it does a fantastic job of telling the story of how technology can slowly, effectively, and unknowingly shift one's perspective until they're fully radicalized. The creators of the movie have founded an entire organization, called The Center for Humane Technology, devoted to the "mission to drive a comprehensive shift toward humane technology that supports our well-being, democracy, and shared information environment" (Center for Humane Technology, n.d.-b).

On their website, The Center for Humane Technology provides a large variety of resources for navigating social media and developing media literacy, such as First Draft News (now part of the newly formed Brown University Information Futures Lab), a resource for combating misinformation and identifying reputable sources of information, and brain science on how social media "hacks" our brains (Center for Humane Technology, n.d.-a). These resources are a great foundation for bringing media literacy awareness to yourself, your students, and your classroom.

Final Thoughts

As a society, we should reflect upon our collective stereotypes regarding our attitudes toward the importance of visual communication. My personal experiences working with early elementary learners has demonstrated and reinforced the effectiveness of visuals as a Universal Design for Learning strategy that can support students across language barriers and reading proficiency levels. By using visuals as part of a larger toolkit to help enhance and simplify communication, we can make our teaching clearer and more effective.

Visual elements can often give clues about the reliability of sources. We've been living in an environment of misinformation and disinformation long enough now to fully realize the impact that visual media can have on our opinions and emotions, polarizing friends and family, and causing viral content to spread, unchecked. This illustrates the dire importance of visual and media literacy for our students, and the need to question and check sources before allowing outrage and sensationalism to take over and risk sharing false and/or misleading information.

The way you set up your classroom (both physical and digital) can have a positive impact on student engagement, culture, and motivation. Relationships and classroom culture are key to building and improving upon social-emotional learning, which in turn opens the doors to deeper engagement with content and curriculum. When students feel welcomed and safe, they are unencumbered by distractions and other hierarchical needs that may impede learning.

Chapter 10
The Impact on Educational Leaders

Ben Dickson

Illustration by Elsa Anderson

Introduction

Unprecedented, pivot, new normal, contact tracing and a host of other phrases I thought I'd never be saying or hearing. Welcome to leading during a pandemic. If you would have told me twenty-five years ago when I had just left working a skate shop to take on a night custodian gig while trying to get my teaching degree that we'd be here today, well you know the answer to that. Twenty-five years ago I had two tiny kids at home and an amazing wife who said, "Hey, let's become teachers." We've never looked back since. To say my educational career has been varied is an understatement. First as a custodian in an elementary school then through thirteen years of teaching Kindergarten through sixth grade and a number of schools. Spending two years serving at a district level as an instructional coach for twenty-one schools opened my eyes to so many different styles of leadership beyond my time as a classroom teacher. This time helped formulate the beginning of my educational leadership journey.

Prior to my education career, I'd "managed" others but running a skateboard shop full of teens and twenty-somethings was vastly different from leading an entire school. Moving from school to school to support teaching and learning, leading staff development, supporting schools with developing their year-long performance plans, analyzing student data, and all the other parts of my unique position showed me so many different ways of leadership. Even those leaders who led in a way that I never would have taught me something about how to support a school, or not support a school.

After a few years of doing this job, I had the opportunity to be part of a turnaround school. This peculiar elementary was going through a "forced leadership" change i.e. remove current building leadership and place new leadership in the building, which involved adding two instructional coaches which included myself.

I'd already been through this process during my teaching career. Prior to leaving the classroom, I was part of a changeover in another elementary school. My principal was tasked with taking over another elementary school and as part of the process changed over 50% of the staff and I was part of that change. To say that the process was rough is an understatement. As a staff member coming in and replacing other teachers, we were not always welcomed. During that short time, I quickly learned how relationships can either make or break a system.

I joined this staff along with the new principal, a new dean of students, and another coach who was a great friend and mentor to me. Again the importance of relationships was at the center of my mind. I knew that we needed to make sure we built strong connections with the staff, families, and students and the four of us worked tirelessly to overcome the perception of being "invaders here to make everyone better because they sucked." This sounds funny, but it definitely was the underlying feeling in many buildings where a forced leadership change occurred.

It was also at this point that I began to work with a national group called America Achieves. My two-year fellowship with this group not only deepened my knowledge of instruction but again showed me a variety of leadership styles as well as put me in contact with so many amazing educational leaders from across the country. Through this work, I began to develop a state-level social media platform to support Nevada teachers and saw my own path opening up to building leadership.

I started my second master's program in Educational Leadership and became the Dean of Students at two elementary schools, spending half time at each one. I was pushed headfirst into the other side of school leadership, the world of paperwork, discipline issues, parent and staff meetings, and less and less of the instructional world I had come from. I realized that school leadership was truly a balance between multiple agendas as well as many competing forces eager to have their "thing" be part of the building.

During this whole journey, my wife was on an educational leadership journey of her own. She also had traveled the path of building instructional coach, dean of students, assistant principal to leading her own elementary school as a principal. As she traveled this journey, she was and continues to be my greatest mentor. Through her eyes, I saw all the struggles and triumphs of leading a building and again the importance of strong relationships.

As with many principals, at this point, my journey to building-leader followed a pretty familiar path. I was a Dean of Students for another year and then moved to Assistant Principal at another elementary school in my district. For those keeping track, I was on to my eighth school, not counting my time at a district level. I joke that my resume looks like I can't

hold a job, but the truth is that these different schools gave me the opportunity to learn from so many different leaders, those with the formal title
and those without. All of them helped formulate my ever-growing view of
school leadership as well as that core belief of the importance of relationships.

This brings me to now, leading school during a pandemic. I started my
first year as principal at the beginning of the 2019 school year, with the
normal triumphs and pitfalls that befall a new principal. But this radically
changed in the spring of this school year when we all went out for our
spring break only to not return to our building for the rest of the year. To
say this caused a radical shift in the way my school looked was an understatement. Teachers were forced to reevaluate what teaching looked like as
we ended the year and I realized that my leadership was being stretched
way beyond anything I had imagined. And again relationships were at the
center of our "new normal."

How Has Educational Leadership Traditionally Been Viewed?

The role of educational leadership has evolved over time. Early on
educational leadership was focused on more managerial roles. Many of us
of a certain age have a hazy recollection of our school principal. Were they
in classrooms? Did I see them outside? What we probably knew was you
didn't want to visit them. Outside of schools, educational leadership was
focused on making sure things run smoothly

Fifty years ago there were movements towards linking the role of
school leadership and learning. The focus began to shift from the manager
to the instructional leader. School leaders, specifically school principals,
were seen as a necessary component to ensure student academic success.
The Effective Schools movement of the 1980s focused on the importance
of the school principal and their role as the instructional leader. Strong
instructional leaders, it was argued, ensured that schools would have the
best chance of success.

The role of the educational leader in any building took on a more critical role as our educational system navigated the changes of the No Child
Left Behind (NCLB) era. School leaders were often praised and criticized

depending on the metrics of this time period. Many a principal was moved due to their schools' ability to perform on tests to the point that large-scale cheating came to light.

At this same time, schools began to see the need for not just an instructional leader in the building but a leader who addressed all aspects of an organization. School leaders began to look more closely at successful leaders beyond the world of education. A school of thought began to form that there were lessons to be learned from the private industry when it comes to leading people. School staff began to be viewed not as employees to be managed but team members to be valued. Teacher leaders, those classroom professionals who by their nature, were seen as leaders in a building, were brought to the forefront and looked at as a valuable resource.

School leaders began to see the need for creating clear Mission and Vision statements not just at a district level but at a school level. Districts and schools began to openly engage all stakeholders, including students, in decision-making processes. While there have always been district-level committees made of community members and school staff, school leaders began to actively seek out community input on school-based decisions.

Community and family engagement also began to be discussed more and more as the School Improvement Grants, starting in 2010, came into play. Educational leaders found themselves flush with cash but had to make some radical changes, including removing school leaders and teachers. These grants stipulated several steps for community engagement through the process but in their quest to get the money quickly most states essentially ignored this principle and received their waivers regardless and the timelines necessitated by these grants left little to no time for community involvement in the decision-making process. Due to this, school leaders found themselves with the mandate to create substantial school reform but often faced a less than enthusiastic group of stakeholders.

School leadership and specifically the role of the individual school principal has evolved through these years to include not only the role of a manager, instructional leader, and community outreach liaison. School leaders find themselves not only ensuring the educational well-being of students but providing support systems and guidance for families beyond the school. School-based leaders often find themselves sitting one moment with district and school staff creating a shared vision for their school and the next helping a family negotiate community-based social services. Schools and districts with successful leaders and in turn, successful schools understand that school leadership is made up of many different facets and skill sets beyond the traditional education role. The most successful leaders find they cannot lead alone and that their role can change on any given day.

Best Practices in Educational Leadership

When we look at what the most impactful practices of successful educational leaders, we can find a wealth of information and while educational leadership can encompass a broad range of job descriptions, I'd like to focus on the role of the individual school leader, the principal, as this is the one that I have the most experience with and one could argue has the most direct impact on students, staff, and community. Jimmy Casas argues in his book *Culturize* that "ineffective leadership is the biggest issue facing not only public education but small businesses and large companies alike" (p. 6). Research has shown that effective leadership in schools shares some common traits. There is a clear focus on the "why" of everyone in the building and each person can articulate what their organization, be it central office, maintenance, or a school site is all about. Effective leaders create this vision by first and foremost creating a positive culture focused first and foremost on strong relationships.

Relationships in education are nothing new. As I sit here typing this, you can google Relationships in Education and get 7,310,000,000 hits and if you just look at just articles termed "scholarly" this number is 5,300,000. Ask any educator what the most important thing is in their classroom or building and my guess is the majority will answer with relationships and if they don't, then you might want to run. But an effective leader cannot rely on relationships alone. Effective leaders build a strong culture where relationships are the core but a group of people who trust and care about one another is nothing without a purpose and vision.

With these strong relationships, effective leaders can then focus on what Michael Fullen and Joanne Quinn describe as the tools for achieving coherence, that shared purpose and call to action that leaders must instill within a system. Fullan and Quinn (2016) argue in order for effective leadership to achieve this coherence they need to incorporate several steps:

- Purposeful actions and interactions
- Build capacity
- Provide clarity
- Create a precision of practice
- Provide transparency
- Monitor the progress along the way
- Provide continuous course corrections when needed

Effective leaders must make sure they are able to create not just a culture of learning but a collaborative culture where learning continues. Through the use of Professional Learning Communities (PLCs) staff can begin to focus on those key drivers Fullan and Quinn talk about. I find that once my staff is able to have that clear vision of what we want students to learn, here is how we will teach and assess that learning and this is what we will do when students either get it or need more support, the stress level is lowered. The PLC process allows educators to realize they are not an island in their classroom but are part of a larger group of educators focused on a common goal. A common goal that must be clearly defined and continually refined to ensure the best possible educational outcome for all students.

Along with this culture building and development of a clear and coherent vision educational leaders are often encouraged to challenge the status quo. When we look back at education over the last hundred years there are many arguments made for ending the "we've always done it this way" mentality. Leaders must have a desire and call to challenge practices that are not effective or fly in the face of building a strong culture. Research on leadership makes the case that effective leaders must be willing to "have a desire to make something happen, to change the way things are, to create something that no one else has ever created before" (Kouzes and Posner P.17). These leaders have the ability to look at problems and present opportunities for teams to come up with new ways to solve them.

Strong school culture built with trusting relationships was key as I entered my first year as principal. I also worked hard with my staff to create a clear, coherent vision of what we wanted for students. We spent many days prior to the 2019/2020 school year going through team building, getting to know and trust one another, and crafting a strong PLC culture within our school. Staff met weekly to look at data, analyze their teaching, and look for ways to do things differently when we didn't see the results we wanted. All in all, things were going pretty well prior to March 2020.

How Has COVID-19 Impacted the Future of Educational Leadership?

Once the initial shock of the spring of 2020 and the reality of COVID-19 had sunk in, I found myself having to really rethink my role as an educational leader. As a school, we had to adjust and "pivot" to move to a whole-scale online instructional model. Teachers found themselves teaching online when they had little to no experience doing so. We as a system began to worry less about academic needs and the social and emotional needs of not only our students and families but our staff. We spent that last part of the 2020 school year just trying to keep our heads above water and make sure that our students as well as ourselves remembered to breathe.

The start of the 2020/2021 school year found my district in a different position than most. We opened our school for face-to-face learning for students but also with an online option. We also found ourselves having to navigate mask mandates, social distancing protocols, and an intense focus on safety that had never been done before. This was not school as normal, but it was our new normal and I found myself as the educational leader questioning my own effectiveness.

Instructional leadership was and is still key for me, but I found that we as a school, and I would argue as a system, must make sure we are focusing on the basic needs of our stakeholders. As any psych 101 student will tell you, if a person's basic needs, think Maslow's Hierarchy of Needs, are not being met then those higher-level tasks can never be accomplished. As we moved into the first full school year of the pandemic, we quickly realized that learning cannot take place if safety isn't addressed. We found that students and families who were worried about housing insecurity, jobs, the well-being of loved ones, and other critical needs were never going to be able to focus on learning. At the root of this, schools had to make sure they were providing a safe space for students and families. This meant solidifying and, in some cases, rebuilding relationships and creating a school culture that addressed not just academics but the social and emotional needs of all stakeholders.

Effective leaders cannot pay lip service to school culture any longer. The relationship between teachers and students, teachers and teachers, and that a leader has with all stakeholders must be strengthened and maintained in order for the education system to weather the pandemic. A basis of trust, trust that a student will be safe, that a staff member will be safe, and that all those in school have the tools they need to be successful can only come about once the culture is addressed. Once this culture of trusting relationships is built, only then can school and school systems address the changes that COVID-19 has brought.

Educational systems must now focus on creating structural systems to address student health, and while this always was the case it is now at the forefront. Systems to identify students who may have tested positive, structures to communicate to families should there be an outbreak, tools, and mechanisms to provide tech to students to address the learning, what "distance learning" will look like, and what structures need to be in place to allow students access. On top of all this is the structural change to the school itself. How is the education leader of a building ensuring that health mandates are being followed? Our education leaders now have to shift focus to ensuring social distancing is taking place not only in the classrooms or school hallways but in the lunchroom and possibly on the playground or sports field.

We are in a time of what Anthony Muhammad calls "Technical Change" (p 15). Changes that affect the tools and mechanisms that allow education to function efficiently. These technical changes were always present but as we deal with the new reality of COVID-19 and its effect on education, we have to recognize the technical changes are in danger of overwhelming Muhammad's second form of change "Cultural Change." Systems must be in place to allow schools to run in this new normal but not at the expense of culture. Leaders must continue to provide a coherent vision for schools while supporting a healthy culture.

School systems that have a healthy culture at their root will better cope with these systematic changes necessitated by the pandemic. School leaders that have formulated a culture of trust will find that students, families, and staff are better able to deal with technical changes such as new school schedules, social distancing protocols in classes and buses, and temporary exclusions of students during the school year. These cultures will also support addressing the new normal of education. An educational world that still needs to prepare students for life beyond the thirteen years they spend in school but also the whole child as well. As school leaders, how will we address all the aspects of our job? We will still need to focus on building those strong missions and visions for our schools, but we must also realize that we have many more pressing issues than test scores or graduation rates.

School leaders must be addressing not only the physical safety of their stakeholders but the mental safety as well. As we move through the pandemic schools will find more and more that the trauma of COVID-19 is playing out in untold ways with our students, families, and staff. How are students and families dealing with a year of online school now that they are back in person? How will schools address the different learning styles now that we have seen some students thrive online while others struggled to even attend? And what percentage of a school day needs to be allocated to address the social and emotional needs of students now that we've seen the need for it? School leaders are going to find themselves balancing not only their traditional roles but having to adapt to a new one as well.

Final Thoughts

We are seeing a paradigm shift in what it means to do "school" with the changes of the pandemic. While we will always be in the business of academics, schools are finding themselves having to address the whole child as well as the whole adult. Schools cannot only be a place of learning but also a place of healing for students. Schools can provide a culture where a student knows they will be safe, and that someone cares about them.

School systems that have a healthy culture at their root will better weather these systematic changes necessitated by the pandemic. School leaders that have formulated a culture of trust will find that students, families, and staff are better able to cope with uncertainty and change. Managers will never make it. You may be able to manage through things like exclusions, mask mandates, and social distancing but you won't manage your way through collective trauma and system-wide change

Anthony Muhammad wrote that "the primary problem in a toxic school culture is an inability to properly respond to challenges and adversity" (p. 18). This has never been more apparent than the time we are living through right now. Educational leaders who have taken the time to support and nurture strong cultures are going to find their path less rocky. Schools will face any number of problems including individual health concerns, public disagreement of health and safety policy, lack of access to educational resources due to school exclusion, students and adults in trauma, and a host of other issues, and those that can navigate this will succeed. The future is uncertain but one thing that is certain is that strong cultures focused on a clear vision for students, families, and staff will come out of this stronger than ever.

Chapter 11
Embracing Online Courses
Matt Jacobson

Illustration by Genovia Graham

Introduction

I've always been a tinkerer. I love figuring out how things work, how smaller elements work together to make more complex things. It was a necessary skill on our farm. You see, when you live on a farm, there are always problems to solve on a daily basis, but you rarely have the luxury of resources to call a specialist to solve your problems for you. You learn to figure things out on your own, or with the help of your friends and neighbors.

I'm not a plumber, but I can fix leaky faucets and install toilets and shower valves. I'm not a carpenter, but I can rough together wall studs and floor or ceiling joists and make some simple structures to get a job done. I'm not a landscaper but I can fell trees and redirect drainage and create some nice planting beds and vegetable gardens.

I learned these skills by watching my dad, then by reading books. Dad is gone now, so when I want to learn something, I search for videos and websites that address the problems I need to solve. To be honest, I think these are things that anyone can do if they simply have the desire to learn and experiment, be willing to fail sometimes, but always try again until you get it right.

In my opinion, there are two kinds of educators: those who had a great experience with their own education and feel a calling to continue creating positive learning experiences for others, and those who had a poor to average experience in their educational careers and vow to create better experiences for others in the future. I had a decent small-town, public-school education in the 1970s and 1980s, but college truly opened my eyes. I had some good teachers at university and some really terrible lecturers. Those separate terms, "teacher" and "lecturer," are used quite deliberately. It was obvious that the lecturers were there to publish their research and were forced to lower themselves into a classroom from time to time. I vaguely recall the gen-ed American History class I had right after I had filled my belly with dorm cafeteria lunch when I struggled - often unsuccessfully - to stay awake during the instructor's monotone droning. Others, however, were there to support further innovations in their field by helping others learn their craft, preparing them to help solve problems they didn't know existed yet.

Not long after securing my first teaching position, coincidentally in a middle school American History classroom, I was allowed to attend a professional development conference for new teachers. I fell in love with professional learning. Hard. I begged my principal for professional leave forms so I could learn more about the art and science that is teaching. People told me that I was doing a decent job, and evaluations reflected that. A few teachers complained that I was going to too many workshops. Others complained that my classroom was too loud, that we did too many projects, too many simulations, too many experiments, and too much role-playing. When our standardized test scores came back, often higher than expected, I was accused of "teaching to the test." It didn't matter to us. We were having too much fun learning.

Throughout my career, I've had a number of titles, but the one I feel most comfortable with is that of "Teacher." I've helped traditional junior high teachers learn to be high-functioning middle school team teachers. I've spent over a decade coordinating professional development and technology training for a school district. Currently, I'm called the "Online Learning Coordinator" for the Learning Technology Center of Illinois. That simply means that I help other educators learn online and help educators develop online and blended learning opportunities for students in their schools; and, if I can't help them do that, I find someone who can.

I'm a teacher. My classroom is your computer. My students are anyone who can access the Internet. These days, yours are, too.

How Have Online Courses Been Viewed Traditionally?

After spending more than a decade-and-a-half in the business of helping educators learn and grow, I can confidently say I've learned a few things through experience. Here are a few of the myths that need to be dispelled.

Myth #1: "Teachers need professional development." With all due respect to Dr. Nick Sutton's recent publication, *Make Professional Development Matter*[1] I firmly believe that the terms, "professional development" and "teacher training" need to die. It's called "Professional Learning." Teachers have already been trained for at least four years and further developed through the unpaid internship called student teaching.

Telling experienced, degree-holding educators that we are not sufficiently developed or that we require more training after all of that is not simply offensive to every college and university that grants degrees to educators, it is a slap in the face to the individual and to the education profession as a whole.

Myth #2: "We can all do a little more for the <insert your school's name here> Family." Educator self-care has been ignored far too long. Teachers spend the weeks leading up to the start of school decorating their rooms for their students. We spend our own hard-earned dollars on supplies. Teachers spend their evenings grading papers and weekends lesson planning. Often, we must take on an extra part-time job to support our families. (Been there, done that.) On top of that, teachers are then asked to stay after school once a month or more to attend the school or district's "professional development meetings." We're told that, while we rarely see our own actual families. In my experience, school leaders who offer teachers the luxury of choosing topics of their own interest, or allow them to pursue that learning at a time and pace of their own choosing, have been hard to find.

Myth #3: Learning online isn't good quality learning. I have worked in districts that would not recognize online degrees, provide salary scale advancement for online coursework, or place student teachers who were enrolled in online-only degree programs. The reasons I heard most often revolved around the perception of poor-quality educational programming, the perceived inability to confirm that certain prerequisites were truly met, and the bad reputation that a few fly-by-night "colleges" had cultivated. While that stigma may have held true a decade or two ago, the online professional learning experience can be extremely valuable today, especially to our younger educators. More about that a little later in this chapter.

Myth #4: You can just "put your class online." We are still learning more every day about the science of learning and the art of teaching in traditional brick-and-mortar settings. For years, at least in my experience, professional learning for the average classroom teacher focused largely on those things. Learning online was something that only the teachers in alternative settings had to deal with. In the classroom, we can work face-to-face with our students, get down on one knee to help a student figure out a question or problem, redirect a student's attention with proximity cues, and so on. We can see and "feel" (I don't know what else to call it) when kids are "getting it" much better or at least more easily in person. We have all learned during the pandemic that learning online is a completely different beast. During the nationwide remote learning experiment of the last year-and-a-half, we educators suddenly had to first figure out the physical and virtual nuts and bolts of computer-supported teaching and learning. Designing instruction differently, interacting with students differently, and assessing learning outcomes differently all took a back seat to figure out if our cameras are on or if our mics are muted. While we have been focusing on the hardware and software associated with learning online, it seems to me that relatively little attention has focused on designing instructional experiences and student interactions differently in the online space. The same can be said for the professional learning provided to teachers. Designing instruction differently, interacting with students differently, and assessing learning outcomes differently have all taken a back seat to figuring out if our cameras are on or if our mics are muted. While we have been focusing on the hardware and software associated with learning online, relatively little attention has seemed, to me at least, to focus on designing instructional experiences and student interactions differently in the online space.

The Best Practices of Online Classes

Teachers Learn Best When They Choose Their Professional Learning Paths.

Schools and educators are under increasing pressure to pursue learning outside of their choosing. This may be the result of efforts to protect schools against legal action to the efforts of legislators to achieve or retain elected office. According to research compiled by Lieberman and Wilkins (2006)[2], "professional development for teachers has gone from a choice to a mandate," during the past decades.

According to research by Seto (2016)[3], "...personal choice of professional learning should be supported in school change efforts... Schools seeking improvement efforts could set a particular topic goal, give educators the freedom to pursue their own learning, then host a sharing event to see what varied learnings come back. The sharing out of professional learning with colleagues who pursued the same topic can be valuable..." (p. 84)

- The quality and effectiveness of online professional learning experiences for educators has improved.

According to Darling-Hammond, et al.[4], "effective professional development [is defined] as structured professional learning that results in changes in teacher practices and improvements in student learning outcomes." The United States Department of Education's Office of Education Technology (2014)[5] has stated that the highest quality online professional learning experiences share these seven characteristics:

- Supports active rather than passive participation
- Is grounded in empirical theories and models of learning
- Aligns purposefully with student outcomes as well as individual educator and organizational learning goals
- Is engaging and relevant
- Is paced and timed appropriately
- Is led or designed by skilled online facilitators
- Establishes a set of norms for participation

The same article outlines and includes rubrics for evaluating several different types of online professional learning opportunities. These include

- Webinar: Synchronous web-based events hosted via video conferencing software
- Hashtag Twitter Chat: Prearranged Twitter status updates that are organized around a specific topic and are linked together by hashtags to create an online conversation
- Online Conference: an Internet-based version of a more traditional professional learning conference or convention that allows the audience to participate virtually and/or in-person

- Online Course: a specific set of learning objectives or outcomes that are supported with online learning tools, activities, or experiences. (self-paced or facilitated)
- M.O.O.C.: a Massive Open Online Course that allows a very large number of participants to engage with course materials and activities online
- Online Community of Practice: a group of educators organized around a specific educational practice who share and discuss ideas and experiences through the use of online tools to advance their collective knowledge.
- High-quality online learning for educators can be designed and delivered locally to address specific learning paths.

According to the United States Department of Education[6] online learning for educators is growing dramatically. A 2019 study by The Learning Accelerator[7] indicates that educators perceive the following six elements to be critical drivers of quality online teacher professional learning experiences.

- Platform Quality - refers to the ease-of-use of the online tool(s) used to deliver professional learning experiences
- Rigorous Content Focus - refers to the connection between appropriate relevance to both the educator's subject expertise and the school or district's goals
- Active Learning - refers to ways the professional learner engages with the content, their own prior knowledge, and with other professional learners.
- Mastery Learning - refers to the level which the professional learner displays their understanding through practice, assessment, and feedback
- Connection - refers to the ways the learner integrates new knowledge with their previous understanding and the understandings of others.
- Personalization - refers to the ways that the professional learner sets their own goals and proceeds through the professional learning content

Even the most experienced educators still like to learn. Teachers have earned the professional degrees needed to supervise children and write curriculum and lesson plans. The truly professional educator can self-identify needs and paths of study that will benefit the students they serve. If that is a foreign concept administrators or colleagues can provide options or coach them to select areas that can help them improve. Providing educators with opportunities to pursue the learning that most interests them, on their own terms, and be recognized and rewarded for the growth they demonstrate, can result in amazing experiences for the professional educator and the students they serve. Well-designed online learning opportunities allow the educator the agency they both want and deserve.

How Has COVID-19 Impacted the Future of Online Classes?

Internet searches for recent articles about online teacher professional learning and online teacher professional development yield a surprisingly ancient list of results. Most of my searches for scholarly publications or professional journal articles provided results from 2010 and before. As this is being written at the end of 2021, it is hoped that others will pick up the banner of research into the topic of post-COVID online teacher professional learning soon. However, a few generalizations from my personal experience and existing research can be shared confidently at this time.

A growing menu of free and low-cost professional learning options are becoming available to educators. Sure, lots of businesses have sprouted up that offer individuals, schools, and districts professional learning solutions, both online and in-person, and charge fees that range from nominal to the outrageous. Their sales pitches are designed to make us believe that they can solve all of our problems in the nice, neat package that they have each designed and will deliver over the course of a school year or longer. But if a quick video online or an hour-long course can do the same thing for free, why are we wasting educators' valuable time with still more pointless meetings?

To take advantage of the research and ideas presented above, just a few steps are needed to change the professional learning narrative in your school or district.

1. Collect data about students' academic and social-emotional needs and present that data to teachers.

2. Create a school or district professional learning plan using the data shown above.

3. Ask teachers what they want to learn about. A simple survey using free online form creation tools can make this relatively easy and anonymous.

4. Allow teachers to create their own professional learning plans that include observable and achievable goals that are linked to student outcomes.

5. Administrators and teachers can work together using published evaluation tools to adjust personal professional learning plans to ensure quality and alignment with the needs of students in their school and district.

Final Thoughts

During the pandemic, we all had to become tinkerers. We all had to find problems that we didn't know existed and figure out solutions. Some students and their teachers embraced this as an opportunity to redefine how education looks and feels. Others struggled with this new manner of learning, and some dug in their heels and longed for the days when the old ways of teaching and learning would return. Whether or not we use online learning well will be debated for years to come, and the results of this "grand experiment" will vary greatly from classroom to classroom and from school to school. But what did we really learn?

1. The mental and physical health of both students and staff must be our first priority, whether we serve others from a classroom, an administrative office, or a board room.

2. Learning how to learn online is new for both adults and students, and it takes time to adjust.

3. Streamline the learning to focus on and reinforce the basics. Focus on the "need-to-know," rather than the "nice-to-know."

4. Think about smaller learning events rather than recording sit-and-get lectures. This is good advice for both student learning and professional learning activities.
5. Adults and students alike will benefit more when provided choices in the mode, method, and pace of learning.

Last, some advice: Failure is only the beginning. You may have seen a social media meme stating something like this:

F.A.I.L. = First Attempt In Learning

This is very true. You may feel like you have failed when learning online because you don't "get it" the first time through. Failure is uncomfortable. Accept that you may feel uncomfortable when learning something new in ways that may be unfamiliar. Don't give up, and don't be afraid of it. The human body's physical reactions to fear and excitement are nearly identical: increased heart rate, quick and shallow respiration, maybe a little sweat on the brow, and so on. What separates the two is how we choose to perceive the situation.

Chapter 12
Remote Instruction
Professional Development

Brian Bates

Illustration by Blair Bates

Introduction

I remember when finishing my master's degree and earning my administrative license, I told my wife several times that I was not interested in jumping into an administrative position right away. Though I had been teaching for six years, I felt like I was more than ready to take the leap into a leadership role. That role, however, would need to be an absolute perfect situation for me to leave my middle school science classroom and give up coaching seventh-grade girls basketball. Little did I know, a few weeks later, that perfect situation would show up, leading to an interview and eventually being hired as a middle school assistant principal. But it didn't take long to realize that this wasn't the leadership role I was seeking.

As my first (and only) year as an assistant principal wrapped up, I found myself heading back to the middle school classroom, teaching sixth-grade math and science. Even though I loved teaching, I still felt that I had something more to give. I was lucky to join a school that had just piloted a 1:1 Chromebook program the previous year and was expanding it to all grade levels. I found ways to use technology for modeling in math and science, using hyperdocs, flipping my math class, and eventually moving towards creating a self-paced math curriculum. I had embraced technology and was anxious to find new ways to engage my students. And that's when the connection was made.

I was asked by the high school assistant principal in my district to come and demonstrate to teachers how I was flipping my math classroom and the video tools I used to make it possible. It was my first time presenting something of my own to my peers. I had a few presentations under my belt, but those were "train the trainer" and, to this point, had never shared my own thoughts, ideas, or examples. This day had a profound impact on my career as I had finally found that role I had been looking for all along. By the next school year, I had transitioned to a role as a professional development coordinator for a consortium of two Regional Offices of Education in west-central Illinois. This experience led me to my current role as a Director of Professional Learning for the Learning Technology Center of Illinois (LTC), a program that provides support to all public K-12 schools in Illinois with instructional technology.

As I look back on my career path, it's hard to believe I ended up in a role focused on educator professional development for the past five years. What's strange is after my first experiences with teacher professional development, I should have been turned off to the idea of ever being in this position in the first place.

How Remote Instruction Professional Development Has Traditionally Been Viewed

I walked into the gym and found a place at one of the cafeteria tables. They were those old folding tables that once you were more than four feet tall, you had no business sitting at. It was my first time attending a school inservice day as a student teacher. After the speaker was introduced and they began their presentation, I got out my notebook to take notes, like I thought the other teachers were doing. But I scanned the cafeteria and when I looked closer, I noticed those teachers that I thought were taking notes were actually grading papers. There were a few teachers actively listening to the speaker, but most were engaged in other activities. The session wrapped up and everyone headed to lunch before an afternoon of team and personal prep time.

While at lunch, it became obvious why so many in the cafeteria found other things to do during the morning professional development session. I heard comments such as "Why did I need to be there this morning? I teach *(insert subject here)* and this has nothing to do with me? That all sounded great in theory, but has it ever been done in a *real* classroom? Don't worry, by the time we start school next year, we'll have a new initiative to focus on." As a student teacher, I wondered if these statements were true. Reflecting back at this point in my career and remembering that morning I can say without a doubt those teachers all had a valid point. It hit home for me more in the next few years as I got a teaching job and had my own classroom. I felt the frustration as another teacher institute day came and went. I found myself repeating the same thoughts that those teachers had when I was a student teacher.

From the Classroom to the Workshop

To understand why the professional development mentioned previously, or any other traditional form of educator professional development fails, look no further than our traditional classroom practices. Many teachers, including myself, passed through an educational system that looked relatively similar. Students were sat in rows and columns facing the chalkboard. The teacher spent the majority, if not all of the class time, talking in the front of the room while students took notes. More recently, the teacher might have some type of slide show presentation to display as they lecture. Other times, students read silently or aloud from a textbook with the teacher pausing to ask clarifying questions. If students were lucky, there might be a few minutes at the end of the class period to start working on homework before the bell rang. Throw in a test or quiz every few weeks, maybe a project each semester, and that basically sums up a traditional educational experience for many.

It's no surprise that the individuals designing and delivering professional development, usually current or former teachers, create these experiences with traditional teaching methods in mind. The instructional practices are simply transferred from their classroom of students to a cafeteria or auditorium full of adults. It is not uncommon to participate in a professional development session for educators where the presenter stands in the front of the room and talks the entire time, fervorously clicking through slides in a desperate attempt to cover all the content.

Traditional teacher professional development is ineffective because it fails to address one or more of the three main issues.

1. It does not relate to the teacher and/or what they do in their classroom.
2. It does not engage the teacher as an active participant.
3. It does not provide the teacher with adequate support.

Why Am I Learning This?

This was a question that my students asked me frequently, and rightfully so, early in my teaching career. The responses are embarrassing to think about now. Needless to say, they were poor responses and I wish I had known then what I came to know down the road. Later on in my career, I shifted away from following the textbook and the traditional approach of assigning problems or worksheets. I realized that embedding math skills, such as unit rate and operations with decimals into activities and projects like planning for a road trip, resulted in fewer times I was questioned on why we were learning these skills. The same is true for teachers. One of the quickest ways to lose the attention and interest in a professional development activity or program is by not clearly articulating the purpose of the activity to the teachers. If the professional development does not relate to what the teachers are doing in their classrooms and they are not able to make connections between the professional development content and their own work, then you've already lost them. Furthermore, many teachers are required to sit through professional development sessions that are not even relevant to what they teach. While there are some topics, such as social-emotional learning and competency-based education to name a few, that impact all teachers, many times the professional development is focused more on the core curriculum. When the purpose or relevancy of the professional development activity is not clear and obvious, teachers are less likely to buy into the professional development.

The Sage on the Stage

Another unfortunate characteristic of traditional teaching practices that has spilled over into teacher professional development is the lecture format, or "sage on the stage" as it is often referred to. Many presenters, like some teachers, will stand at the front of the room and share their knowledge by clicking through a slideshow (and in some torturous cases, read word for word from those slides) while sharing their expertise. While in some cases, and in small doses, this may be a necessary minor part of teacher professional development, it often becomes the only strategy used by the presenter. Thinking back to my first example from my student teaching experience, by not actively engaging the teachers in the cafeteria that day, the presenter allowed the participants to shift their focus to other things, like grading papers. Fast forward to the present, every teacher now has a smartphone and/or laptop in front of them. Passive professional development that does not require the teacher to take an active role in their learning allows that teacher to use the time to catch up on parent emails, update their grade books, plan out the next week's lesson, or even just scroll through their social media feed.

A report from The Learning Policy Institute (Darling-Hammond et al., 2017) found that traditional professional development often fails to provide teachers with the opportunity to learn new skills and strategies by actively trying them during the professional development session. Passive professional development doesn't just provide an opportunity for the participant to check out and be distracted by work or technology. It fails to provide an opportunity for teachers to practice new skills or use new strategies before incorporating them into classroom instruction.

One Hit Wonder

Finally, traditional professional development mirrors our traditional instructional practices in that feedback and continuous support are not always provided. Traditional workshops, institute days, even large conferences for that matter, offer a "one and done" approach to professional development. The speaker swoops in, runs through the PowerPoint, answers questions, collects their round of applause, and heads to their next destination. The audience either got it or they didn't. Teachers may actually walk out feeling excited and prepared to try something new they have learned. But without the support and feedback, the excitement and courage to try something new may soon vanish. Think about how this looks in a traditional classroom. How often do teachers (and I admit to doing this in the past) present a new skill or topic and move on to the next without proper support and feedback? I can think of times where I gave my students a test at the end of the unit and found their scores to be overwhelmingly low. What did I do to support their learning? How much time did I spend providing explicit feedback to them? Oftentimes, teachers get caught up in how much needs to be covered and the timeline for doing so, and we fail to take the time to provide the appropriate support for our students. The same can be said for presenters. It becomes more important to get through all the slides than to provide a deep, meaningful learning experience.

There are certainly other issues with professional development that are not mentioned here. And while this section has cast a negative shadow on professional development, there are certainly many presenters and professional development providers out there that have mastered the art of designing impactful and effective professional development. What is it that they've figured out that others have not?

Defining the Best Practices of Remote Instruction Professional Development

Professional development is a necessary part of education and, when it includes a few basic elements, can create impactful instructional change and most importantly, improve student learning. A quick Google search will provide numerous articles, blog posts, and journal entries with any number of "top tips" or "essential strategies." The Learning Policy Institute study (Darling-Hammond et al., 2017) identifies the best practices listed in this section for effective professional development. What is effective professional development, actually? In the report, the authors define effective professional development as "structured professional learning that results in changes to teacher knowledge and practices, and improvements in student learning outcomes." It is important to note that effective professional development does not only mean the teachers improve their skills, but it also translates into improved student learning.

Focused and Job Embedded

As mentioned previously, in order to achieve buy-in from the teachers and for them to understand the purpose for the professional development, it is crucial that the program is focused on the content they teach. What's more, it should not just be content-focused, but job embedded, meaning the learning has a direct link to what the teachers are doing in the classroom. The Learning Forward Standards describe a vision for job-embedded learning. In the standard "Learning Design," job-embedded professional development is done during the school day and includes activities such as reviewing student data or case studies, conducting peer observations, teaching simulations, conducting action research, or even student observations, to name a few (Croft et al. 2010).

Promotes Active Learning

One of the other issues with traditional methods of teacher professional development mentioned in a previous section is that many times, the workshop or session is simply a person reading from their slides. Participants are expected to gain knowledge and skills simply by listening and retaining information without actually interacting with the content. Effective professional development provides numerous opportunities for the teacher to be engaged with their learning. Active learning provides more opportunities for sense-making. I have often heard teachers say, "Sure, this sounds great in *theory*, but what does it actually look like in the classroom?" What better way to put theory into practice than with active learning? Active learning is often an umbrella term that includes several of the next best practices.

Collaboration

Educators all share the responsibility of teaching the students in the school community. It makes sense to think of teachers as a team. One of the most important things that a team can do is work together. Collaboration in professional development helps teachers grow and improve their instructional practices as a team, which will improve learning for all students. Collaboration may look differently in various professional development settings. Teachers may participate in book studies, have a common planning time, participate in learning walks or lesson studies. One of the most effective forms of collaborative professional learning is professional learning communities (PLCs). Huffman and Hipp (2003) define PLCs as "a school's professional staff members who continuously seek to find answers through inquiry and act on their learning to improve student learning." Effective PLC's share six main components: shared mission, vision, values, goals; a collaborative team focused on learning; collective inquiry; action orientation and experimentation; commitment to continuous improvement; and results orientation (Dufour 2006).

Modeling

When coaches see their players shooting a basketball incorrectly, the most common way to address it is by modeling the correct form. The player watches the coach shoot the jump shot correctly and then makes changes to their own shot. Why should it be different for professional development? Modeling in professional development might include watching recorded lessons, live lessons, or even peer observations. Modeling is equally important when implementing new teaching strategies or curriculum changes. It's not enough to just hand a teacher new curriculum or have them read a book on a new instructional strategy. Just like the coach telling the players how to shoot a basketball, showing them the correct way is also important.

Coaching and Expert Support

Coaches are individuals partnered with teachers that help them analyze current instructional practices, set goals, and provide support in planning and designing instruction to achieve those goals. Coaches are highly effective, and research has found that instructional coaching promotes the learning implementation and accountability. (Annenberg Institute for School Reform, 2004). Coaching is a support that responds to the ongoing needs of students and teachers in a structured method. This only works if there is a mutual respect and trust between the coach and the teacher. This is why this method can be much more effective than peer feedback and observations.

Many schools struggle to find enough teachers to fill open positions. So hiring a coach may not be something that is a possibility for them. It doesn't mean that the coaching support cannot be used in their buildings. Oftentimes, professional development providers offer ongoing support after initial professional development activities as a way to help with this issue.

Feedback and Reflection

What is the purpose of formative assessment? Ideally, formative assessment provides a system for teachers to give feedback to their students during the learning process and use corrective measures to make sure they address any misconceptions and evaluate how they can improve their instruction to help the students learn. This is an absolute necessity for teacher professional development as well. In one-and-done workshops, teachers are exposed to new knowledge and skills and are turned loose to try them on their own. But what happens when it goes wrong? What happens when the outcomes aren't what they expected? This leads to teachers being frustrated and giving up. Building in time for peer educators, coaches, or even professional development providers to offer feedback to teachers is critical for successful implementation.

It's not just enough to receive feedback. The teacher must take time to reflect on the feedback given, review the professional development knowledge and skills, and make the necessary changes to improve their instruction. Oftentimes, teachers are their own worst critic and by reflecting on their teaching practices, they are able to identify strengths and areas for improvement.

Sustained Duration

In the Effective Teacher Professional Development report (Darling-Hammond et al., 2017), the authors mention that there has yet to be any research to indicate the ideal threshold for effective professional development. They do, however, note that of the over thirty professional development programs studied for the report, none of them included "one-and-done" activities. It's often been said that to learn a new skill it takes ten thousand hours. Josh Kaufman, author of *The Personal MBA*, has said that it only takes twenty hours (Schawbel 2013). While there is no perfect answer, those designing and delivering professional development programs must ensure there is enough time to successfully implement the best practices listed above.

How COVID-19 Has Impacted the Future of Online Instruction Professional Learning

Classrooms and education in general looked very different on March 1, 2020 compared to April 1, 2020. In some ways, it may never look exactly the same again, and that may be for the better. But not only did the pandemic change the way educators taught, it also changed the way they learned. Teachers across the country and all around the world were asked to teach their students in ways they have never tried before. In a survey by The Christensen Institute (Arnett 2021) 8% of teachers stated that they used live video instruction prior to the pandemic but 68% responded that they were using live video instruction during the pandemic and school closures. In the same survey, 22% of teachers had created online lessons for their students pre-pandemic. During the pandemic, 51% of teachers were creating online lessons. These drastic changes in designing, creating, and delivering instruction happened overnight. What did these changes mean for teacher professional development? How did they prepare for this shift?

The Most Timely, Job Embedded Professional Development

As mentioned in the earlier section on best practices, professional development is most effective when it is timely, focused, and job embedded. If a global pandemic causing the closure of schools across the country doesn't trigger a need for the timeliest professional development, I'm not sure what else would. School districts without fully implemented 1:1 technology programs in place frantically scrambled to get devices in students' hands as quickly as possible while teachers began the task of learning how to shift to a world of teaching completely online. They needed to learn, and they needed it now. As schools began reopening, teachers have still been seeking out timely, relevant professional learning. The pandemic has shown both professional development providers and teachers the importance of offering professional development at a time that is convenient for the teacher and with a delivery method that meets their needs.

Virtual Instruction Calls for Virtual Professional Learning

With seemingly everything in the world closed down, including schools, how were teachers going to get this desperately needed and time-sensitive professional development? Just like teachers, professional development providers shifted to virtual learning as well. While most professional development still came in the form of workshops, conferences, and district in-service days, virtual professional development has been growing even before the pandemic. Webinars, virtual workshops, podcasts, and social media were the new normal for teachers in the pandemic. But as schools closed and teachers needed help, these methods became the lifeboats for supporting educators. Teachers could join a webinar, watch someone (often a fellow teacher) demonstrate how to organize and distribute activities through Google Classroom, and then go and do it themselves immediately. Live or pre-recorded virtual professional development allowed teachers to find exactly what they needed to learn and see it modeled for them. Self-paced online courses provided teachers the opportunity to learn on their own time, especially if they had their own children at home while they were also teaching.

New Pathways for Continued Support

Not only does virtual professional development give teachers the ability to learn anytime, anywhere, but they also can receive the ongoing support that is so crucial to the successful implementation of new skills. Since presenters no longer have to travel to reach their audience, they can schedule follow-up sessions by simply sending a calendar or Zoom invite. It can be easy to meet with teachers or groups of teachers by scheduling a virtual call during their plan time. This way the presenter doesn't have to give up a full day just to meet with a few teachers. Even as some professional development activities are returning to in-person formats at the time of this writing, many are still utilizing the idea of virtual follow-up sessions. It reduces the amount of travel time for both presenters and teachers, eliminates the concern of cancellations due to weather, and brings the overall cost down for the participants.

Final Thoughts

Reflecting back on my first experiences with professional development, one thing was an absolute constant. Professional development was something that was always done to me. What I mean is, someone decided what I needed to learn, how I needed to learn it, and when I should learn it. I was not given a voice on my own professional development. At a time when teachers are seeing the power of offering student voice and choice in their classrooms, the same needs to be extended to teachers. No longer should they sit through professional development that isn't relevant to them or doesn't meet their immediate needs. Consider what this might look like to professional football quarterback Tom Brady. Does he become one of the greatest quarterbacks of all time by spending his practice time working on tackling? Does he participate in field goal kicking practice with the other kickers? Absolutely not. Not all football players need to work on the same skills. Neither do teachers. Teachers must be allowed to select the professional development that they need, at the time that works best for them, and a delivery method that fits their learning style. The pandemic required teachers to seek out the professional development that they needed to do the best they could for their students. I believe that moving forward, teachers will continue to seek out and participate in virtual learning opportunities that meet their needs and make them even more successful in the classroom, be it physical or virtual.

Making Teacher Professional Development More Equitable

Teacher voice and choice sound great in theory, just like many other educational initiatives. During my early years of teaching, I was able to participate in district in-service days, usually two to three days per year, and a one-day conference at a nearby state university. If I asked to attend anything else, the first question was always, "How much will it cost?" Even though the question was always asked, I felt like the answer was already predetermined. I will admit, I understand that school budgets are already stretched very thin, and many times sending a teacher to a workshop or a conference might not appear to be the best use of funds. At the end of the day, you can have the safest school, with the most advanced technology and the best-designed learning spaces imaginable, but if the teachers aren't pushing themselves to be the best at their craft, does anything else matter? Shouldn't we do everything we can to help teachers learn and develop new skills and strategies to be able to reach all learners?

The global pandemic, in my opinion, has expanded the opportunity for teacher professional development and has made it more equitable for teachers. When the world shut down, those who provide professional development learned to adapt. In-person sessions became virtual. A workshop series became an asynchronous online course. New series of webinars were developed, hosted after school hours, and made on-demand. State and national conferences were hosted online on virtual conference platforms. Teachers had the option to join these virtual professional development opportunities at their convenience. And in many cases, the virtual aspect made the activity free or low cost. For example, many conferences were held virtually in 2020. To attend those types of conferences before the pandemic, it might cost anywhere from $500 - $2000 depending on travel distances and duration. But now in a virtual setting costs were able to be drastically reduced, making it much more affordable for teachers to log on and participate in the learning. Not to mention the fact that no subs would be needed since the teacher wasn't needing to travel. It wasn't just cost barriers that were in the way before the pandemic either. Workshop series and conferences are often hosted in larger, more heavily populated areas. I totally understand why event organizers would do this. Their goal is to fill to capacity, so they go where the most people are. I can tell you that spending almost all of my career in west-central Illinois, it gets frustrating to have to travel the three hours to Chicago or St. Louis for a conference. I can only imagine what it must feel like to someone even farther south in the state than I was. Since everything was being hosted in a virtual setting, your zip code no longer mattered. There was no need to drive in the day before and get a hotel room for a one-day event. Teachers weren't forced to drive several hours just to have the same opportunities as other educators. At the Learning Technology Center of Illinois, we saw teachers from all over the state and all corners of the country join our virtual professional development activities. There were even several international teachers!

While the devastating loss and political divide that has been a result of the global pandemic is something I wish never happened, I do believe that it has shown the power of virtual professional development for teachers. Teachers are able to access professional development that is timely and relevant to their classroom instruction, models active learning in a virtual setting, provides support and feedback in a sustained program, all while being available to them on their time at their convenience by removing significant barriers to accessibility.

Chapter 13
Best Practice Remote Instructional Strategies
Ben Sondgeroth

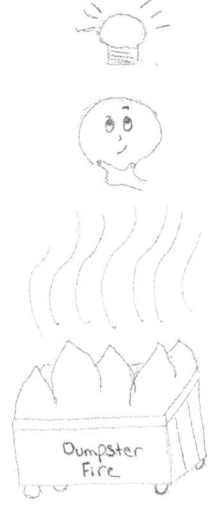

Illustration by Addi Sutton

Introduction

My name is Ben Sondgeroth, and I am currently the Lead Regional Education Technology Coordinator (RETC) for the Learning Technology Center of Illinois (LTC). As a RETC, I provide services and support in all things educational technology for the districts in Northwest Illinois. My professional experience has had me on quite a journey. In 2009 I graduated from the University of Indianapolis with a degree in History Education to become a social studies teacher and baseball coach. I achieved this goal when Morrison High School in Morrison, IL hired me in 2010 to become one of the school's two history teachers and their varsity baseball coach. While Morrison is a small district of only one thousand students, this decision would significantly affect my educational technology journey.

As a second-year teacher, I was provided a class set of Apple iPad 2s, and one of two teachers in the district was given the opportunity to learn how to use these devices in the classroom. That year, my goal was to reinvent my curriculum to all digital and online information and go completely paperless. It was certainly a year of learning, and a year that would lay the groundwork for me as a future educational technology professional. It would lead to a foundation of skills that I still use to this day when helping teachers discover best practices of teaching with technology.

After teaching with the iPads for three years, I transitioned into the role of Director of Technology for the district. During this time, I oversaw the deployment of over nine hundred Chromebooks in grades three through twelve. This was in 2014 when 1:1 was still a very new concept and one that we did our best to manage. We knew that teachers needed as much professional development (PD) as we could offer, and a large majority of that PD became my responsibility. At this, I found an immense passion for helping teachers discover the best practices for integrating technology into their curriculum. While my teaching experience was limited to just a high school experience, I found immense joy in working with all grade levels and discovering technology's power in the classroom.

This passion continued to grow when I joined the educational technology company EdTechTeacher in 2016. EdTechTeacher's mission is to support educators in their quest to enrich student learning experiences through technology and innovative models of classroom instruction. During my time with EdTechTeacher, I traveled the country to work with and learn from thousands of teachers as they embarked on their edtech journeys. During this time, I worked with some of the brightest minds in the educational technology space and developed new and innovative ways to utilize technology in the classroom.

Now, working for the LTC, I'm happy to be working in my home state with teachers from the region I live in. With the LTC, I've been able to work with thousands of teachers from across Illinois on best practices with integrating technology, and during the school year of 2020, at the height of remote learning, we were never busier. As an organization in FY21 (July 2020-June 2021), our team of ten people provided training to over nine thousand educators. Much of this time was spent working with teachers on how to best utilize the technology they had available to meet the needs of their students in a remote learning environment.

Since the pandemic started, I have learned a lot about how technology can be effective in remote learning environments. I've also held a tremendous amount of respect for educators that have had to deal with the challenging circumstances in transitioning to teaching with technology and in a remote environment. This chapter will dive into remote learning best practices, and I'll use my experience working with teachers to make the best of an extremely difficult situation. I consider the work that the LTC and I did from the spring of 2020 and forward to be some of the most rewarding work of my career. I know I learned a lot working with educators on developing best practices in remote learning, and it was extraordinary to see many of the teachers I worked with take the practices that we worked on and apply them with their students. While remote instruction on a mass scale may be over, I will be using this chapter to explore how we can take remote instruction's best parts and continue to utilize them for the benefit of our students.

How Has Remote Instruction Traditionally Been Viewed?

When addressing the traditional view of remote learning, the use cases in K-12 are relatively limited. While there are certain instances of remote learning that were taking place prior to the start of the pandemic, much of the attention on technology in schools was focused on in-classroom instruction.

There were instances when remote instruction and learning were taking place before the pandemic, and in those instances, many of the schools that were doing this were very forward-thinking in how they could assist students in need. For example, the Morrison School District, where I worked previously, established a system as far back as 2012 to support students away from learning for extended periods. One instance involved a high school female who had given birth to her first child. The student did not want to fall behind on her classes while staying at home with her new baby. The technology department issued her an iPad with Skype added to it, and in her core classes of math and science, they set up an additional iPad that the teacher could use to Skype her into the classes live.

Four years later, a freshman student suffered a severe injury during a football game that bound the student to a wheelchair for several weeks. This instance happened after our district had moved to a 1:1 environment with Chromebooks and adopted Google Apps for Education. We provided the permissions on the student's account to access Google Hangouts and set his teachers up for him to video call them at the start of every class. He was able to successfully video into his classes for the few weeks that he could not physically attend.

I don't think any of us knew that what we were doing then would become the norm for educators only a few years later. Reflecting on the experience, I think it shows that the technology to do a lot of what we accomplished during the pandemic at the K-12 level has been there; it simply takes creative minds to maximize it during a crisis.

The areas where remote learning and instruction held ground before 2020 trended towards higher education. Teachers and other professionals have been attending online graduate courses for years. My own master's degree was obtained through the University of Illinois in 2013 through a hybrid learning experience. Our cohort of teachers would all meet on

Monday nights via the collaborative platform that we used and listen to our professor lecture on the topic at hand. We would also share our screens and presentations with the group. It was truly a great experience that was very much ahead of its time.

High school students have also historically been afforded the opportunity to learn remotely by taking college-level classes. The format of these classes varies greatly depending on the university offering them. Many are designed as asynchronous learning experiences for the students. My experience with a class of this nature dates back to 2003-2004 when I took an online math course through our local community college. It was certainly a very early iteration of remote learning as there were limited videos and limited contact with the professor. However, it allowed us the chance to receive college credit for a math class our high school was unable to offer.

States have also previously offered the opportunity for students to learn through virtual schools offered by states as alternative options to brick and mortar schooling. These virtual schools have a somewhat controversial reputation as their success rates are lower than brick and motor schooling. In the paper "Bricks and Mortar vs. Computers and Modems: The Impacts of Enrollment in K-12 Virtual Schools", Carycruz Bueno finds that "that attending a full-time virtual school leads to a statistically significant reduction of between 0.1 and 0.4 standard deviations, in English Language Arts (ELA), Mathematics, Science, and Social Studies for students in elementary and middle school" (Bueno, 2020). Bueno also argues that students who return from a virtual school to a traditional school recover fully from their drop in test scores. A common theme why these virtual schools have a record of poor performance comes from the lack of engagement with students and the lack of a physical teacher in the learning environment. It is not all doom and gloom in the virtual school world as many students do find success and much of that depends on the virtual school that is chosen and the support that the student is receiving at home. In the article "K-12 Virtual Schooling, COVID-19, and Student Success", the authors argue "individual students need to be motivated, organized, and supported. Differences in their environment, meaning their access to instructional support as well as their internet access, can cause significant variations in student success" (Black et al., 2020, #119). In the next section, we will address strategies and tactics teachers can use in a remote learning environment to combat these challenges.

To examine remote teaching and learning's traditional viewing is difficult as it was not something that would be considered prevalent in mainstream education. Before the spring of 2020, I imagine a small percentage of educators would have ever thought they would be teaching students that were not physically in front of them. Technology use in schools was prevalent, but the strategies used by teachers were not focused on remote instruction and instead focused on using technology to enhance learning for their students. Similarly, access to technology was not available for many schools and students. While many schools and districts were undertaking the implementation of technology, many were still waiting or financially unable to afford the devices and infrastructure to support a proper implementation.

Similarly, access to devices and connectivity at home was something that many schools and districts did not have to worry about before the pandemic. The conversation in Illinois was starting to trend towards a discussion of what "e-learning" days would look like. The state legislature had passed a law allowing schools to implement e-learning days in the instance of school closures for weather or other reasons. Since this was happening, some schools were beginning to recognize that if they did implement an e-learning day, not all students would be able to complete fully online activities. However, since these days would be limited to only using a few per year, teachers could make accommodations quickly for those students.

As you can see, the topic of remote teaching and remote learning is very young, and the term that we all heard far too often of "unprecedented times in teaching" was very accurate. So, where do we go from here? When writing this, we have nearly two years of experience in implementing remote instruction. Studies have been done examining what the best practices are and how we can improve teaching with technology moving forward. In the spring of 2020, there was not much to go off of, and many teachers were simply trying to support students as best as possible. Now we can rely on best practices and help our students learn while they are remote.

Defining the Best Practices of Remote Instruction

As we look at what defines best practices in remote teaching, we have to look at the foundations of the problem. Our problem during the spring of 2020 and the school year of 2020-2021 was focused on schools being closed and teachers being forced to teach remotely. From this, there have been many studies on what constitutes the best practices in remote teaching, albeit from my perspective, it is a short timeframe to fully understand what effective practice is and how we can measure it as such. With this in mind, as we explore these best practices, we remember that good practice in remote instruction can often be good practice in teaching with technology in our traditional classrooms. So while teachers may not be teaching remotely anymore or if they are it is more than likely in short stints or in a hybrid classroom (one that serves both students at home and students that are in the physical classroom with the teacher), we can apply the best practices explored here outside of the framework of a fully remote environment.

To that end, we will look at how we best create an environment where our teachers are supported as they are teaching remotely. As discussed previously, many teachers had either never used technology in their classrooms or had used it in a more traditional classroom setting. In fact, according to a survey by GBH Education, "only 66 percent of teachers reported being very or extremely confident in using digital media services for teaching, and 1 in 7 had not previously used K-12 digital media services" (Ferren, 2021, 5). As a professional development provider, I can say that at the beginning of the COVID-19 pandemic, many teachers were not ready to teach in a remote environment. To support this, schools need to provide teachers with the services and support they need to understand what it means to be an effective remote learning teacher. Too often, teachers in a remote instruction environment attempt to recreate what they have always done in the classroom. Schools were guilty of this, often making students and teachers follow the same bell schedule for remote instruction as they would during a regular school day. We can look to two reasons why this happened in our schools: a lack of professional development on leveraging technology effectively and a lack of time given to teachers to develop new ways to engage students remotely.

In talking to teachers, a lack of time is perhaps the most critical factor in their lack of change in teaching style when moving from traditional to remote instruction. Teachers feel overwhelmed and stressed by the circumstances they face, and we certainly have to have empathy for them. In order for change to occur, it falls on leaders in schools to find a way to provide teachers with additional time to refresh and reconfigure their curriculums to work more cohesively online. This can take many different forms; Thomas Arnett of the Christensen Institute recommends, based on their findings, that leaders relax "required instructional days and minutes and developing assessment and accountability systems that prioritize student well-being and growth in mastering content" (Arnett, 2021, 13). One of the keys to success is to make sure that the time given is used appropriately and not wasted.

It is essential to provide teachers with high-quality professional development when given this time. As a person who provides hundreds of hours of professional development every year, I find that while large group professional development can reach a more significant number of teachers at once, it is often not the most effective way of sustaining change. Similarly, providing professional development to staff for a singular day or afternoon will not elicit real change in their practices. My organization, The Learning Technology Center of Illinois, believes in this so strongly that we have created an instructional technology coaching program that embeds coaches into districts to work with teachers on best practices. This model of sustained professional development and sustained contact with teachers aims to continue to encourage teachers' growth in their practices.

I recognize that the coaching model may not work for every school, as access to a qualified coach is not something widely available. With that in mind, there are strategies that schools can use to maximize the staff they have to train and coach their colleagues. For example, schools can build up a network of model educators within the buildings or districts to work with other staff to promote best practices. Schools can also find online professional development that focuses on the most effective methods of educating students remotely. As stated by Arnett, "When the survey asked hybrid and remote teachers to report their sense for how well they are able to serve their students, those who felt confident with online tools and those who felt they had received effective PD were substantially more confident than hybrid and remote teachers generally" (Arnett, 2021, 11). Schools must not forget to continue to provide ongoing professional development for their teachers and give them the time needed to develop strategies and practices that are best for their students.

The question then becomes what type of practice teachers should use when developing curriculum and content for their students in a remote learning environment. The Christensen Institute believes that teachers have an opportunity to build student-centered learning environments while teaching both remotely and with technology in the classroom (Arnett, 2021, 7). I am a big proponent of this thinking as well. A student-centered learning environment allows students to take ownership of their learning while freeing up the teacher from conducting full instruction to students who may have trouble staying focused on a video call. When we put the power of learning into the student's hands, we open up their ability to engage with the content in a way that works for them. Now, student-centered learning is not simply handing the keys to the car over to the student; the teacher still controls the objectives and often the content. However, they empower the students to explore and demonstrate their learning in ways that work. Technology allows us to make this happen as students are not bound to one textbook and are not bound to one method of demonstrating their learning.

So what are some of the best practices for student-centered learning in a remote environment? One way is for teachers to record their lessons and instruction in short, smaller sizes for students to review on their own time. These lessons can be taught synchronously and recorded in real-time to prevent the teacher from repeating the same work multiple times. I encourage teachers to break these videos down into short clips before posting to a Learning Management System (LMS) or another content delivery platform. In doing this, we allow students to take a break from watching a very long video and process what they have learned in small bits.

The strategy of short sessions can be also applied to our youngest students that may be in a remote learning situation. For our younger learners, it is important to keep synchronous sessions short and allow them to participate in activities that are away from their screens (Norris, 2020). While this student-centered learning style may be different from how it looks for older students, when we allow the students to complete activities, we are helping them develop independence. Admittingly, this can be a challenge as remote instruction with our youngest learners relies heavily on parental assistance. To that end, it is a best practice to make sure your parents are also supported, and they have the tools available that allow them to be successful with their children. The LTC provided this support for parents in creating the Supporting Parents and Remote Kids (SPARK) program. The program aims to give parents of remote students the resources they need to navigate the online learning tools their children are using. In leveraging support resources like this, schools can make the remote learning experience for the family a better one. Schools should look to develop a parent support database on the tools used in remote instruction. In making the database readily accessible to parents, you provide a resource that will increase the success of learning for your students.

In a more detailed approach to student-centered learning, teachers can also look at innovative ways to engage their students with technology. It is essential to remember that these best practices can be applied in a remote learning environment or a traditional classroom setting. When engaging students, teachers can create choice boards using tools like Google Slides or Google Drawings. In a choice board, teachers can provide their students with multiple options to pick from in their learning. Each choice will lead to a source that could be an educational game, video, reading material, or even a podcast. These choice boards provide the students with multiple pathways to gain the knowledge they need on the topic they are covering in class.

Teachers can also use technology to create a station-rotation experience for their students. In a remote learning situation, teachers can leverage the power of breakout rooms in a product like Zoom or Google Meet. Each breakout room asks the students to complete a different task with their peers, and after a set period of time, the teacher can call the student back from the breakout rooms to rotate into a new breakout room. Teachers are more than likely familiar with this style of instruction in a physical classroom; it is important to remember that even in a physical classroom, students can still participate in a station-rotation activity using the technology that they currently have available. They may not even have to rotate and can virtually jump from station to station from their desks!

Another great strategy that promotes student-centered learning in a remote environment is creating and using HyperDocs. A HyperDoc is most commonly built using a Google Doc, but you can accomplish many of the same strategies in a Microsoft Word document as well. In a HyperDoc, teachers curate information for the students to engage and learn from. Often these HyperDocs will include links to outside resources or activities for the students to complete. The students then use the Google Doc to document their learning or reflect on what they have learned. It is important to distinguish that a HyperDoc is not simply a document with hyperlinks in it. Instead, it is a living document that students can collaborate on and curate their learning with their peers. To learn more about HyperDocs, I encourage you to visit the HyperDocs Gals website at hyperdocs.com.

While remote learning is not a perfect environment for students to learn, it was our reality for many months. We can take away many lessons learned from this time and use these best practices to make future remote learning situations the best they can be for our students.

How Has COVID-19 Impacted the Future of Remote Instruction?

When we look forward to what the educational landscape will look like coming out of the COVID-19 pandemic, I believe we will see a long-lasting impact on connecting students to information that previously was not available. The baseline for technology use in the classroom has been established. Teachers of all ages and experience levels, at one point or another during the COVID-19 pandemic, had to utilize technology and learn how to implement it with their students. The usage level was not universal, nor was it used by all to its fullest potential, but now we can build off this baseline.

We have an opportunity in our schools to encourage teachers to take the next steps in utilizing technology for innovation and teaching their students the skills they will need in the future workforce. Our students have also been exposed to more technology than they would have previously. This allows them to engage with technology academically, rather than simply using it to consume media and other miscellaneous information. While we see students as digital natives and of an age whose world is centered around technology, they often do not know how to use technology to create and curate information. The pandemic has provided an opportunity to educate our students using technology on a broader scale and provide them with access to new and exciting possibilities.

As previously stated, the future of remote learning and technology in the classroom will allow students to access content that may not have been available before. A student in rural Illinois can now take college courses from a university in a different part of the country, all from their own home or perhaps during a designated class period in their school day. The previous iteration of this class may have been very self-guided and contained only asynchronous learning opportunities. Now, with the gained experience of remote instruction, universities can redesign these classes to include both asynchronous and synchronous learning for the student. We can only imagine that for many students, gaining the option of an asynchronous learning environment will improve their ability to grasp the content in front of them better.

Similarly, schools can now connect with one another, providing an opportunity to pool resources to best educate their students. Should a school face a teacher shortage, forcing it to cut classes or programs, that school now has the opportunity to collaborate with neighboring schools and share teachers. For example, a district may be short a Spanish teacher and unable to offer Spanish classes to their students. With the experience of setting up classrooms for streaming lessons live during the pandemic, the schools could collaborate to share a Spanish teacher who streams into one of the classrooms daily. Many schools purchased cameras, microphones, interactive displays, and more to allow their teachers to stream their classes during remote learning; we must think creatively about utilizing these resources best moving forward.

Coming out of this, teachers also have the opportunity to reinvent how they are teaching. I see and hear many educators talk about burnout in the teaching profession. It is understandable, and this was taking place long before the COVID-19 pandemic happened but has certainly been expedited by it. When we look at the impact of remote learning and the increase in technology in our classrooms, we can encourage teachers to bring new resources and voices into their curriculums and classrooms. An incredibly positive way to avoid burnout is to mix up a long-lasting routine of doing the same thing day in and day out, a routine that many teachers fall into. This will not be easy, as routines can be comfortable and hard to shake and add in the potential for the new technology to fail and risk teachers slipping back into the mundane routine and burnout. When this happens, schools need to be supportive and provide opportunities for teachers to explore the technology but not in yet another how-to webinar or demonstration professional development. Allow them to remix lessons and the support and time needed to build new content and activities with their students. Pushing teachers toward new and innovative ways of teaching and using technology is not easy. However, innovation often comes from chaos, and the COVID-19 pandemic has caused chaos in our educational system. We now have an opportunity to create innovation and change the educational system for the better.

Final Thoughts

Coming out of the COVID-19 pandemic, teachers have an opportunity to shift the way educational content is fundamentally delivered to our students. While remote learning was far from perfect, it did show us that some students do have the ability to learn anytime and anywhere. The content and courses offered in our brick-and-mortar school buildings no longer have to be the only content that our students are subjected to. With the increase in technology accessibility, our students and teachers now have an entirely new world of content and resources to explore. Our rapidly outdated textbooks no longer have to be the end-all of learning in the classrooms. Students can inquire about subjects and immediately look up the answers to their questions. Teachers can bring in a wide array of new material to their classrooms and virtually share it with their students.

As described previously in the chapter, the abundance of virtual schools and online offerings from universities will provide this and future generations of students with the opportunity to learn subjects they would have never had access to before. It is not the subject matter that remote learning is changing the narrative on, but the ability is now there to connect our classrooms virtually with professionals in various fields of study. Teachers can have university professors join their classrooms to discuss content with their students. Workplace professionals can also join to demonstrate how the subject matter the students are learning correlates with real-world jobs. This is not limited to only connecting adults to our students as classrooms across the world can connect via video conference, and students now can interact directly with other students a world away.

While many of these activities and practices outlined in this chapter have been available for teachers to partake in with their students, the pandemic expedited them. As an educational technology professional, I hope that moving forward, teachers continue to utilize the technology skills and practices they developed in remote learning in their classrooms. While remote learning was incredibly challenging for many, so many positives can come from it. Because of remote instruction, our classrooms have access to more technology now than ever before. The COVID-19 pandemic created more disruption and chaos in our educational system than at any other time in history. As I stated earlier, I believe that chaos causes innovation, and we saw teachers and schools become incredibly innovative during remote learning. Moving forward, let's encourage our teachers to keep being innovative with their teaching and enable them to use technology and remote learning to maximize the ability for students to learn in our classrooms.

Chapter 14
Ensuring Equity Across all Educational Settings

Dr. Kimako Patterson

Illustration by Kaden Bell

Introduction

"On your worst day, YOU are some child's Best and ONLY Hope!" I have had the pleasure of serving children for the last twenty-five plus years in education. My goal has always been to make the classroom, building, department or district better than it was when I arrived. I strive to achieve EXCELLENCE in all things related to a child's experience in school. I am still striving towards this goal, and I would be remiss if I pretended like this isn't a serious challenge. As a matter of fact, there are times when that goal seems downright impossible, but alas, I continue to believe, hope and pray.

I was born into a family of educators. Both my father and my mother taught and were administrators in the Chicago Public School system. All of my aunts were teachers/professors on the elementary, high school, and university level at various stages of their careers. I guess it isn't difficult to imagine my passion for teaching and making a difference in the lives of children. I started my own career as a third grade teacher at J.N. Thorpe Elementary School in Chicago, IL. This experience had the greatest impact on my future career, but I wasn't aware of that at the time. I spent five years as a teacher for the Chicago Public School system. I then went on to serve as an Assistant Principal, Principal, Supervisor of Curriculum and Instruction, and Assistant Superintendent. I wanted to deepen my knowledge of standards, objectives, curriculum, alignment, and assessments. As such, I spent a couple of years working for a private company that specialized in aligning curriculum and assessments to local and state standards. During this time I began to miss children and had a hankering to return to the school building. I felt that armed with my current knowledge and experience, I could make better and more impactful decisions in the best interest of children as an administrator. Let me pause now and reminisce on my naivety. It is always so interesting when I speak to new administrators about WHY they desire to be an administrator. So many of them have that same desire and passion, and it is honorable. However, what I have learned in the many years in which I have been blessed to be an administrator is that the desire without the resiliency, grit, and determination necessary to withstand the challenges and continuously evolve is fruitless. In order to be effective and impactful, one must be able to stand

and withstand, one must be able to strategize and multi-task, one must be able to create solutions to problems and keep children as the focal point always.

In 2011, I became the Superintendent for Prairie-Hills Elementary School District 144 in Markham, Il. In addition to being a superintendent, I have also had the pleasure of being the president of two local and state organizations consisting of superintendents. I mention this because I now know and understand firsthand the frustration that arises out of the desire to make decisions in the best interest of students, and the inherent challenges resulting from local, state, and federal guidelines that impede that progress. It almost feels like I am coming full circle in my career. I started as a teacher with the desire to make differences in the lives of children. I worked hard and rose to the position of Superintendent and while I am able to make more decisions for children in my current position, these decisions and meeting goals for my students have not come without chaos, and confusion. In the midst of all of this I have managed to create systems, policies, and processes to improve the learning environment for all students and staff members. And yet in the midst of it all, the quest for EXCELLENCE requires providing equity in all systems, processes, policies and procedures and this continues to be a challenge, specifically my challenge.

I have had the pleasure of knowing Dr. Nick Sutton for several years, and when he suggested I expound on the challenge of providing equity for all, I jumped at the opportunity. In all honesty, I balked initially and thought, "Absolutely NOT, not me…why me? Find someone else." And as the words were running through my mind, my mouth said, "Yes, let's do it." So we are going to take this journey together as I share my relentless quest for excellence and equity! I do not pretend or proclaim to have all of the answers, or even some of the "right" answers. I absolutely have questions, just like you, and I intend to share my thoughts, ideas, experience and insight to assist all of us as we try to provide equity for all students.

How Has the Topic of Ensuring Equity Been Viewed Traditionally?

In Illinois, the main three educational agencies (IASA (Illinois Association of School Administrators), IASB (Illinois Association of School Boards), IASBO(Illinois Association of School Business officials) combine forces to host an annual education conference. The Joint Conference, as it is called, hosts workshops for all positions in education; board members, administrators, teachers, community members, parents, and support personnel. In November 2021, I had the pleasure of attending this conference with my board members. We attended a keynote session where the speaker was talking about equity and entitlement. He was specifically speaking about selection processes that uphold the "status quo," of how students are selected to various universities in the U.S. The entire presentation was on how some entitlement programs do NOT provide equity, even though they were intended to do so. The speaker went into detail regarding the admission of thousands of students into various prestigious universities throughout this country, and yet when it's time for the universities to close none of them recognize the possibility that some of their students have no place to go or no "home" to return to until the university opens again. He was addressing the lack of equity in upper academia especially for either minority students or those who have less than their peers. It was a sobering reminder of how inequitable our facilities, programs, organizations and structures are in this country. In my opinion, it was an outstanding presentation and spoke to the heart of equity. As I left the workshop, I overheard two men talking, and they stated that the students should be happy they were accepted into the university to begin with. They went on to say that worrying about where they stay isn't anyone else's problem. The final statement blew my mind, and they stated, "Those students should be happy they were offered equity in admissions." I was really stunned for several reasons, mainly because the keynote speaker differentiated the difference between equality and equity when he initially started his presentation. In addition, the lack of concern or inability to empathize with the students and their lack of a place to call home was enlightening, especially when this particular conference is composed of people committed to and dedicated to providing access, equality, and equity to all students, or perhaps not? As I processed the conversation, I was further stunned by the fact that most people really do believe that these two words are synonymous instead of different.

Equality is defined by Websters as "the state of being equal." In contrast, equity is defined as "the quality of being fair and impartial." In layman's terms, equality provides that every student receives the same access, instruction, materials, experience, etc. However, equity provides that every student receives what they need in terms of access, instruction, materials, experience, etc. which may differ from their peers. For example, all of the students in Ms. Smith's classroom receive hardcover textbooks, but one student needs the textbook enlarged electronically, and another student needs the textbook recorded for them. One student has a greater need to see the textbook, and another student has a greater need to hear the textbook. These are clear differences based upon the needs of the students. However, if we work in the constructs of "equality" then we stop at providing all students with a hardcover textbook. If we work within the constructs of "equity" then we provide the textbooks that the individual students need even if those needs differ from others.

It is interesting to note that lately when we discuss equity in education, the topic of race immediately rises to the forefront. The reality is that equity in and of itself doesn't refer to race. In essence, equity refers to providing resources based upon the needs of the individual regardless of race, ethnicity, and culture. Now the topic of racial equity is absolutely intertwined when we discuss equity, because the roots of inequities are typically seen in disproportionate numbers in minority communities. Equity demands that NO learner is marginalized for any reason regardless of race, religion, ethnicity, or sexual orientation.

I would argue that we have attempted to capture equity in various federal programs such as the No Child Left Behind Act (2001), and strategies such as differentiation. The more glaring issue is that we have not created any systemic movement towards really addressing equity because it has become both a political and a racial issue. So the real issue isn't about garnering resources to provide equitable services to all students. The real issue is that so many people simply don't believe. In the book, *Leadership for Equity and Excellence*, authors Scheurich and Skrla state the following, "...If you are going to successfully lead a school to attain both equity and excellence, you first have to believe it is possible." I believe we make assumptions that everyone in the field of education is dedicated to the belief that ALL children really CAN learn and are entitled to successful schools. The reality is that everyone does NOT believe this to be true. Furthermore, there is a plethora of research linking a student's academic achievement to their socio-economic status. And in contrast, you have the 90-90-90 School research conducted by Dr. Douglas Reeves in the 1990s highlighting the fact that poverty really has no impact on learning if we are dedicated to providing equity within the learning environment. In Dr. Reeves' study, the thousands of schools selected had:

- More than 90% of the students were eligible for free and reduced lunch
- More than 90% of the students were from minority backgrounds
- More than 90% of the students met or achieved high academic standards

His research shows great gains accomplished by these schools when they chose to meet the individual needs of their students and focused on core instruction. It is not my intent to debate the argument on either side. There are additional studies that have arisen within the past twenty-five years debating this topic from Karin Chenoweth, Heather Zavadsky, and Baruti Kafeli to name a few. I am only interested in highlighting the inconsistencies that exist within the walls of the classrooms, board rooms and district offices. Authors Scheurich and Skrla ask this pertinent question, "Do I...deep inside where my most firmly held and private beliefs reside—truly believe it is possible in the immediate future to create and sustain schools in which literally all children will be highly successful?" No one knows the answer except the individual answering the question. One of the most difficult challenges to overcome in this world is that of changing someone's belief or value system. My continual task isn't to necessarily attempt to change someone's beliefs, but to challenge the status quo and to suggest..."What if?" I will pursue this thought of "what if" in my conclusion.

Defining the Best Practices to Ensure Equity

In order to begin focusing on equitable practices, the hard work of embracing the brutal truth must occur. Jim Collins suggests in *Good to Great*, that no organization has reached excellence or greatness without first confronting the brutal truth regarding their current circumstances. The brutal truth is that equity exists in pockets and pieces in schools and districts within this country. The discussion of equity has become a hot topic during the twenty-first century, as we have realized that equality in and of itself isn't the answer as seen during the twentieth century. As individuals evolve, it becomes imperative to meet their individual needs related to the learning process. People have varying emotional, intellectual, cultural, and gender orientation needs that cannot be viewed with a one size fits all solution.

Research suggests that there are clear guidelines that can be embraced to address the inequities that currently exist within our school buildings, policies, boardrooms and school districts. The following are a few areas to address:

- Embrace the Truth
- Explore Beliefs
- Academic Expectations
- Accountability Measures
- Community Involvement

Embrace the Truth

The first step towards identifying your system is to embrace the brutal truth regarding biases existing and functioning within the organization. The truth of the matter is that we all have biases whether we admit it or not. The key is to provide a safe, cultivating, and non-judgmental environment where these biases can be discussed and a plan of action put in place on how to move forward with putting these biases behind us. The critical component is allowing people to express their opinion without judgment and embrace a new thought process again without judgment. Typically the best approach is to have an equity audit conducted before the work begins.

This involves all stakeholders and would provide pertinent information for everyone involved. In *Seats at the Table*, by Joshua Emmanuel Gulliam several board members throughout the country provide their unique perspective and opinion on how to navigate racism while addressing equity within their districts. One board member described this process, "As school board members we must focus on policy. In my district, we're allocating funds for an equity audit at every level of the organization....we're currently in the first phase." Surveys are one way to ascertain biases existing in the system. An initial equity audit identifies the strengths and deficits of the current system and provides a game plan on where to begin the hard work ahead. For instance, a curriculum audit would identify any inherent biases in the curriculum work we use within our classrooms. Does the curriculum look like our students? Are we upholding gender bias in our curriculum and not addressing it? I remember observing a lesson years ago in which one of my teachers did a lesson on the varying Cinderella stories from all over the world. I was immediately intrigued as this was a white teacher and she was challenging her students to compare and contrast Cinderella stories from the U.S., Africa and Mexico. The lesson was very interesting, and you could tell the teacher did her homework. However, in the midst of her introduction she immediately identified the boys in the classroom and stated that they probably never heard of Cinderella because they were busy playing football or soccer. Talk about taking a car off the road map with a swiftness. The entire lesson was now characterized by gender bias. The teacher worked really hard to avoid any cultural bias, but she didn't even think about gender bias. There are a plethora of biases existing within each individual and our society as a whole. Our goal is to address them and focus on how to become more inclusive in our current environments. Several states such as Washington, Iowa, and Kentucky provide resources for districts to provide equity audits. Illinois is in the process of preparing these resources to identify and support districts in their own efforts to establish equity across the board.

Explore Beliefs

Exploring a person's values and beliefs is a very tenuous process. Typically they are embedded into who a person is and how they behave publicly and personally. Most people are not willing to share their true beliefs with others who they don't trust or know. As such, professional development regarding beliefs and closely held biases about race, gender, ethnicity, and religion must be identified, addressed and discussed. Our country has long-held beliefs that children of color and poor children cannot learn at high levels. Haycock (2001) discusses this in her research:

"...when we speak with adults, no matter where we are in the country, they make the same comments (about the children who are on the wrong side of the achievement gap). "they're too poor" "their parents don't care" "they come to school without an adequate breakfast" "they don't have enough books in the home." "Indeed, there aren't enough parents in the home." Their reasons, in other words, are always about the children and their families."

It is imperative that we explore the belief systems of all stakeholders within our school communities. Our goal is to help others believe that all children can learn at high levels, but one must first believe this is possible and then commit to the work necessary for this to occur. The research regarding focusing on standards, aligning assessments, providing feedback, effective instruction, and leadership is clear in that it does have an impact on student achievement.

Academic Expectations

We have discussed the importance of conducting curriculum audits to highlight gender, culture, religion, and other biases existing in those materials. The focus should be on a cohesive curricular alignment with state and national standards. This focus should be on a short amount of standards that can be taught at a deeper level. Unfortunately, our current national focus is on teaching a plethora of standards with little to no depth. Assessments should be aligned to the standards taught and students assessed throughout the school year. This provides for short- and long-term assessments, as well as, in-process measures to ensure that students are learning what is being taught. These assessments don't have to be formal. There are a plethora of informal assessments such as exit tickets that teachers can utilize just to quickly assess whether a student understands the skills taught. Collaboration and observation amongst teachers are critical in identifying and discussing student work. We also need to provide culturally responsive teaching within our classrooms. Students need to be able to relate to that which looks like or reminds them of themselves or their families and environments. Ladson-Billings (1994) and Lisa Delpit (1996) are among the most well-respected scholars who discuss the framework necessary to actually provide this teaching within the classroom. This entire process takes time and is critical to student achievement. It must be done on an annual consistent basis in order for the district to remain fluid and in tune with their equity efforts.

Accountability Measures

As previously mentioned, various programs and federal legislation was designed in its intent to provide equity, but the impact has yet to be felt throughout this country. The former U.S. Secretary of Education stated the following in 2002 while referencing the NCLB legislation,

> "Never in the history of human civilization has a society attempted to educate all of its children. Under this new law, we will strive to provide every boy and girl in America with a high-quality education—regardless of his or her income, ability or background."

> — Rod Paige

This emphasis on overall total accountability is critical to student achievement in the past, currently, and in the future. Accountability is the measure used to ensure intent and impact are aligned. We are all accountable for the failure and success of our public school system. As such, it is our collective responsibility to ensure that we do all that is possible to provide an equal and equitable education system whereby all learners are welcome and able to learn.

Community Involvement

Far too many times we view parents as part of the problem and not part of the solution. It is my firm belief that if we invite parents into our classrooms, buildings, and districts as true collaborators then the journey would be different. Parental and community involvement is critical to our students' success in and outside of school. I was raised on the old adage, "It takes a village to raise a child." This actually meant something in the community in which I was raised. We all had a role to play in the success and failure of our communities. When one succeeded then we all succeeded, and when one failed then it was a collective failure. At some point we have gotten away from this collective efficacy and our schools, communities and society as a whole is a result of what happens when we stop working together for the common good.

The Impact of COVID-19 on Ensuring Equity

The impacts of the COVID-19 pandemic will be felt for years to come. It showed a blinding eye on the inequalities and inequities that have existed in educational systems throughout the country and the world. There was a rush to provide technology devices for all students and homes. This appeared to be the easiest task to accomplish initially. However, the digital divide was supposedly being addressed in the midst of the federal NCLB (2001) legislation. Nevertheless, research shows that at the onset of the pandemic 40% of schools lacked broadband services while over twenty-one million Americans lacked an internet connection (America's Digital Divide The PEW Charitable Trusts 2022).

While the focus was placed on attempting to address technology deficits, there was no emphasis on meeting the individual needs of children or adults. Teachers were asked to do herculean tasks of instructing students online and in-person in certain districts. Those teachers who had little to no technology skills were offered crash course training and expected to teach and meet the expectations of asynchronous learning. Students who showed up online were thrust into this new way of learning with little to no support. If the student was fortunate enough to have familial support, then networks were created whereby parents took turns supporting students and their individual needs. Additional tutorial services were also provided to students whose parents had the necessary resources. But for the thousands of students, many but not all of whom were minority learners, there was little to no support at home. Schools were not equipped to attempt to quickly pivot and meet all of the different needs of their students. Some were emotionally disengaged and needed to understand what was happening in the world, but most schools didn't have that answer as the adults were wondering the same thing. Those students who struggled academically and depended upon individual tutorials from their teacher didn't have their needs met at all. Those students who excelled and needed an extra push from their teacher in most cases had to wait for their teacher to work through technology issues, answering questions online from students and parents, and still the teachers were unable to fully challenge those students as they would have within the classroom.

If we were unable to close the equity gap and digital divide prior to the pandemic, then the pandemic has only created a wider chasm between the haves and the have nots. The impacts of the COVID-19 pandemic have been felt on all sides. The 2021 school year has actually been more challenging and volatile than the 2020 school year. We are providing social, emotional, and academic support to all students and yet the toll is still high. It honestly feels as if we are beginning from square one and this could actually be an awakening for all of us. My district and I started this school year "reimagining education." We decided to reimagine what education, instruction, and collaboration should look like within the walls of the classroom and school building. This task is huge and cannot be done alone. In order to produce something different, we must reimagine what could be and focus our talents and attention on creating something new and possible!

Final Thoughts

I remember listening to my parents debate education when I was young. Because they were both educators, there was always a surplus of issues to discuss especially in the 70s. One of my most poignant memories is when my father, Robert Lee McGregor, who has since passed asked me why I wanted to be a teacher and I responded, "I want to make a difference, Daddy," and he asked to whom?? My candid response was this, "I feel that I have been blessed in my upbringing with you and Mom and I just want to be in a position and an environment to pass on this knowledge, interest, and passion." My daddy looked at me clearly and said, "Well, I hope your generation can do it, princess, because I have been in education my entire life and the more things change...the more they stay the same." That thought has resonated with me for the last twenty-five plus years in which I have been in education. My passion hasn't waned, but I have managed to watch an overabundance of programs, strategies, and movements come and go with no real impact, and very little change.

How is it possible that in 2022, we are still wrestling with the same issues and initiatives that I dealt with in the 1970s when I grew up? How is it possible that as much progress as we have made in this country there has actually been little progress made with regard to policies and procedures? How is it possible that our intent hasn't affected our impact or has it? The current educational system was never designed for minority learners, gender differences, or a variance in opinions. It was designed for the haves to continue to grow and rule the have nots. Yet there are thousands of us who continue to fight this faithful fight that the achievement, opportunity, digital, and all other gaps can be overcome or at least minimized.

The words of Ron Edmonds resound with me continuously:

"We can, whenever and wherever we choose, successfully teach all children whose schooling is of interest to us. We already know more than we need to do this. Whether we do it or not must finally depend on how we feel about the fact that we have not done it so far."

— Ron Edmonds, 1970s

Whenever I recite this quote, I am alarmed when I ask myself why haven't we accomplished this task thus far?

Remember I mentioned those what ifs earlier? What if we existed in a society where everyone was committed to the achievement of all students? What if we created an environment where everyone was entitled to their opinions, and we agreed to disagree without being disagreeable? What if we believed that all students could learn regarding their personal circumstances? What if we believed that those students with challenging circumstances could actually learn and achieve at higher rates because of their circumstances instead of in spite of them? What if we just believed that all students had the capacity to learn at their own pace? What if we believed that regardless of gender, race, ethnicity, or religion our country is only as great as its weakest people so we must strengthen the weakest amongst us in order for America to truly be GREAT?!

I could go on and on about those what ifs, but I challenge you, the reader, to not only explore these what ifs but DO something about them. You see, I refuse to NOT believe that the possibility of equity and excellence exists in our school buildings and districts for all students, especially those who are continuously and consistently marginalized. Our children are our greatest resources and assets. Once we truly believe that we can and do impact every aspect of their learning then perhaps things won't continue to remain the same after all of these years...If on your worst day, you and YOU alone are some child's best and only hope...would you take the risk for them to succeed or would you let them fall and fail?

Chapter 15
Taking Risks in Our New World of Education

Kyle Anderson

Illustration by Reed Anderson

Introduction

Perhaps you know me as the tall, lanky kid from high school that was into sports, fishing, and listening to heavy rock 'n roll. Perhaps you know me as the fun-loving guy that loves to laugh and will talk to anybody, the guy many know from college affectionately as Poppy. Perhaps you know me as that tech-loving social studies teacher and coach that always was willing to chat and give you a hand. Perhaps you know me from social media from my Bitmoji giving you two thumbs up on a blue background. Or perhaps you don't know me at all, and this is your first time meeting me.

Regardless, my name is Kyle Anderson. As of this writing, I am no longer the tall, lanky kid, the years have added a few pounds to my frame, but I still love sports, fishing, and heavy rock 'n roll, making people laugh and lending you a hand, regardless of what you may need. I have been an educator for nearly seventeen years, "classically trained" as a social studies teacher, which I did for eleven years. However, if you look at my resume, the first question that you may have is, "Can this guy hold on to a job?"

I started my career, like I mentioned, as a social studies teacher in Las Vegas, Nevada, moving over two thousand miles away from my home state of Michigan in 2005 for my first teaching job. In my first year, I taught United States history and American government, eventually branching out into Advanced Placement (AP) Government, AP United States History, as well as honors sections of United States History. I also was very involved in the extracurricular aspects of my school, coaching football, baseball, and volleyball for several years, as well as serving as an advisor to a ski and snowboard club at my school, taking students that lived in the middle of the Mojave Desert to the snow-capped peaks of Southern Utah and the Sierra Nevada of Nevada and California to experience the snow, for many, for the first time in their lives.

After eleven years in the classroom, I had the opportunity to apply for a district level position as a digital learning coach, a position that would put me on the road traveling to schools to assist teachers in designing lessons that incorporated more technology and innovative practices. After accepting the position, I prepared to step away from the classroom for the first time in my career, but this is where the resume gets a little bit complicated and raises the questions of whether I could hold a job...

First, after packing my things, giving a lot of materials away, and helping the teacher that was hired to replace me get situated, my new position was eliminated due to budget cuts. While I wasn't out of a job, it was devastating knowing how much I was looking forward to a new experience. However, I ended up landing a position at a school that wanted a full-time digital learning coach with a little help from a friend of mine in the district office. This position was very similar to what I would have been doing as a district coach, but after a few months, I felt stagnant and did not believe I was making much of a difference, so I started to explore some other options.

With a few months left in the school year, I accepted a position as a middle school administrator, leaving my coaching position. It was my first position as an administrator and my first role working with middle school students. While I knew the position would be demanding, I grossly underestimated the rigors of a middle school dean. I went from seven to nine-hour days at school to twelve to sixteen-hour days. As an administrator that handled student discipline, very few of my interactions with students were positive in nature, and it took a toll on my mental well-being. Balancing other duties and the limited time I got to see my family drove me to request a return to the classroom after about six months.

The only position available when I asked to leave my administrative position was as a physical education teacher at one of my district's alternative schools, a school for students that had been expelled from their previous school for egregious behavioral offenses. It was a tough assignment, but I kept an open mind knowing that while many students would be hard to handle for a variety of reasons, I knew that I would be home more. However, days were as hard, if not harder, than my short time as an administrator. For lack of a better way to put it, the school chewed me up and spit me out and I have the deepest respect in the world for educators that continue to work in such a tough environment. I knew that I would be moving on at the conclusion of the school year.

In the summer following my time at the alternative school, my family and I moved from Las Vegas to Reno, Nevada so my wife could complete a graduate degree at the University of Nevada (GO PACK!). I would be the sole source of income for the duration of her two-year program and the job hunt was not going well. Ultimately, I was hired by a district as a special education teacher under a contract in which I agreed to earn the credits needed to complete an endorsement in special education for my teaching license. After a few months of completing the coursework (I earned a master's degree in special education in ten months!) and working as a special education teacher, I realized how happy I was that I was as an educator for the first time in a while and was looking forward to many years at my school in northern Nevada.

Upon completing her program and many long discussions, my wife and I decided that it would be best to return to Las Vegas, the city we called home for thirteen years prior to moving north. However, planning to move in the early days of the COVID-19 pandemic proved to be, to put it lightly, almost impossible. Housing was hard to find because of the physical distance between Reno and Las Vegas and the unwillingness, understand-ably, for realtors to show homes. Reserving a moving truck and finding help to move was also another tall order. Eventually, we were able to make the move and after we both secured jobs, we are happy that we made our way back to Las Vegas. I am currently working as a special education teacher, co-teaching algebra, a subject that I never in a million years thought that I would be teaching.

So from the end of the 2015-2016 school year through moving back to Las Vegas in 2020, I have had six different positions: social studies teacher, digital learning coach, middle school administrator, physical education teacher, special education teacher in one district, and special education teacher in another district. Some may look at this as indecisiveness, perhaps even a lack of ability or confidence in my own abilities. I, however, look at the last few years of my career as a period of time where I tried some new things, took some risks, and learned a lot about myself as a person and an educator.

How Risk-Taking Has Been Traditionally Viewed

Just hearing the term "risk-taking" or "risk-taker" can elicit a number of reactions. Even now, my first reaction to hearing either term conjures up images of someone trying something that many would not do, such as skydiving, bungee jumping, blasting down a double black diamond back-country ski trail, or in the maximum sense, going over Niagara Falls in a barrel. However, risk-taking isn't just reserved for extreme sports. Every day of our lives, especially as educators, we engage in some sort of risk-taking, even if you don't necessarily view a decision as taking a risk.

Risk in our everyday lives as educators can be something very simple to an outsider. It could be trying a new lesson activity or technology tool for the first time. It could be asking your principal to attend an out-of-state conference and seeing if there is money in the budget to help you pay for the trip. It could be approaching a colleague or supervisor for help with something, something that you may be hesitant to do in fear of looking incompetent, inadequate, etc. It could also be deciding to stay home on a day when you mentally need to take some time for yourself rather than subjecting yourself to the daily grind.

However, risk can also be something that is drastic and takes a considerable amount of thinking, planning, and courage to do. It could be packing up everything that you own and moving hundreds, if not thousands of miles away from what you have known to start over in something new. It could be deciding to leave a toxic and discouraging work environment, even though you love your students and feel bad that you would be abandoning them. It could be applying for a position that you know that you are underqualified for or have little experience or knowledge about, viewing it as a challenge and setting out to conquer it.

For some people, risk is something that is just a part of their everyday life. Some people view risk as something that you do in the learning process. If you are learning how to skateboard, you assume that throughout the process of learning how to stand on the deck, use one of your feet to propel yourself forward, leaning from side to side to turn the board, and when learning how to do tricks like an ollie or a kickflip, you are going to take some falls and hurt yourself, potentially badly. However, after some falls, cuts, scrapes, and even some broken bones, a lot of people get very good on a skateboard and some even make a career out of it, making thousands of dollars traveling to competitions, the X Games, and now even the Olympics and sign endorsement deals with skateboard and apparel companies. And while I certainly do not view being an educator as being on par with that of somebody learning how to ride a skateboard, there are a lot of similarities.

Each day, you have a choice as an educator to take a risk. It could be trying out a new tool for the first time with students. The whole process could go off without a hitch, or it could fall on its metaphorical face and appear to be a complete waste of time. And if you are reading this, I am sure that you have tried to do something new or innovative for the first time with your supervisor in the room and felt terrible when it did not work out as planned. However, what happens next, regardless of the success or failure that you had with your experience, is what makes the risk worthwhile. If you learned from it and made adjustments for the next time, then it was a risk worth taking. If your supervisor credited you with trying something new and gave suggestions on how to improve, it was worth the risk.

Risk can also be something with much more lasting effects, something that most people would consider a risk when compared to the previous example of trying something new in the classroom and potentially failing. Perhaps you have been an educator for a few years, and while you love going to school each day, passing your passion for your subject area on to students or helping young students learn to read and write, you want to try something new. Perhaps what you want to try is completely different from what you have been doing for years. Maybe it is a position in school leadership as an assistant principal or dean of students. Maybe it is a position as a teacher on special assignment, working with teachers instead of students to assist with technology, literacy, or social-emotional learning and teaching. Maybe it is a position that is not in a school at all but at the district level. Regardless, risking what you have known for most, if not all, of your career can be exhilarating and frightening at the same time. You may end up loving what you do and never returning to the classroom. But you may also end up realizing a short time later that you may have made a mistake.

These types of risks are not ones that most take lightly. Careful consideration, planning, envisioning, etc. go into making a life and career altering risk. Most that go through this process also seek out the advice of their family, colleagues, supervisors, etc. to help them through the decision. One could receive positive feedback and support for making such a big decision, but one could also receive words of discouragement, words that could potentially hinder one from wanting to consider a big risk in the future. Luckily, for most, positive words of encouragement are received with support for their thought process and whatever decision they ultimately make.

Unfortunately, educators do not always work in an environment where trying new things are embraced and encouraged. Many educators have expressed concern for years that their creative abilities are hindered by their school's leaders in the name of standardized testing, community desires (think families that cannot fathom their students not having homework every night), and because "we have always done things this way." Ditching a standard multiple-choice test for a unit assessment in favor of a project, a video presentation, or other student-centered piece of evidence to demonstrate mastery of a concept is rejected by many for a variety of reasons. So instead of trying something new with the idea that student learning could be improved, many educators are handcuffed and discouraged from taking risks in their classroom or school.

In addition, many educators do not have a system of family and friends that are supportive of risk either. While often with the best of intentions, the words of a parent, a spouse, a sibling, etc. can not only be discouraging to try something new, they can be downright hurtful. For example, let's say that one is considering a move into a new district to take on a similar teaching position with an upside to move up into a school or district leadership position down the road. However, in the short term, the move would incur a pay cut and an adjustment to the cost of living. While many may look at it as a move that would require some short-term sacrifice, others may look at it as, "the dumbest thing you could do." If those words came from someone very close to you, that would be very hurtful and discouraging. But the reality is that these types of words and discouragement are uttered from people frequently, contributing to a culture in a family, a circle of friends, or the workplace that is not conducive to risk-taking.

Even risks that are seemingly unrelated to education directly are discouraged from leaders and/or colleagues at times. Over the years, an individual's state of mental health has been brought to the spotlight, with an emphasis on the importance of taking care of oneself, seeking help through therapy, and opening up about struggles with mental health, but even then, many still view those that choose to be vulnerable and open as a weakness that could affect one's performance as an educator. Years ago, after struggling with depression, I sought out the help of a therapist and eventually made a breakthrough with my depression and now have the tools to help me cope better and be more open about my thoughts and feelings. However, when I first went public with my struggles, which was very risky for me to be that vulnerable, most people were very supportive, but a handful of people essentially shamed me for my actions. Luckily, I was able to overcome that discouragement, but not everybody would be able to do the same. If a leader or colleague views vulnerability or risk-taking as a potential liability, it may cause an educator to be less willing to try something new or to be open about risk.

Defining the Best Practices of Risk-Taking

So what does the research say about risk-taking and the impact of risk on educators, schools, etc.? The short answer is... it's complicated. Risk-taking is not a traditional topic of study with scholarly articles published in world-renowned journals chock full of qualitative and quantitative data to fulfill your appetite for research on risk-taking. So while there isn't a plethora of data out there, there are plenty of books out there on risk-taking, its benefits, and ways to motivate yourself to take more risks in your life and career.

One such book is *To The Edge: Successes & Failures Through Risk-Taking* by Kyle Anderson. Wait a minute... Kyle Anderson? The same Kyle that wrote the words that you are reading right now? Indeed, the very one! I wrote *To The Edge* in 2019, published in March 2020 (releasing about a week before the world shutdown due to COVID-19) with the intention of telling my life story of times I have taken risks, the positive and negative consequences of those risks, what I learned from those risks, and how those risks and what I learned shaped me into the person and educator that I am today. My overall goal when writing the book was to motivate others by my story to try something new or do something that perhaps they were afraid to do. And while I could spend the next few pages summarizing my book and presenting it as research, I feel that it is not appropriate to do so. Instead, I humbly ask for you to get a copy of *To The Edge*, read my story, share your thoughts on my words, and hopefully, find some inspiration to do that one thing that you have been thinking about, change your life and/or career direction, and have no fear by taking it to the edge.

So instead of self-promotion, I want to focus on the words and wisdom of three authors and their books: *The 21 Irrefutable Laws of Leadership: Follow Them and People Will Follow You* by John Maxwell, *Drive: The Surprising Truth About What Motivates Us* by Daniel Pink, and *Risk Taker: Strengthen Your Courage, Blaze A New Trail & Ignite Your Students' Passions!* by Brian Aspinall. Of these three books, only one of them, *Risk Taker* by Brian Aspinall, is a book that is focused on educators. The others are focused more on the general population, with Maxwell's book focusing on leaders, but each book has numerous messages about risk-taking, the importance of taking risks, and the benefits of risk.

Let us take a look at *21 Irrefutable Laws of Leadership* first. The author, John Maxwell, has written multiple books, is a successful business leader, and has spoken before large groups of people all over the world, spreading his messages of leadership. *21 Laws* was first published in 1998 and was revised and updated in 2007. While geared toward leaders, the laws are applicable to anyone, in my opinion, and I highly recommend checking it out. For the sake of this focus on risk-taking, I want to turn your attention to three of the most influential and applicable laws of leadership and how they relate to risk-taking: the law of influence, the law of process, and the law of intuition.

According to Maxwell (2007), true leaders and influencers can be measured in followers. Just because a person is in a position of power or has a title of power does not guarantee that they are leaders or influencers. People in these positions that do not influence others to be better are simply managers of human capital and resources, not leaders. Leaders demonstrate impeccable character, build relationships, expand their knowledge, and draw off of their experiences to influence others. While demonstrating these characteristics does not guarantee success, it gives people the ability to give one a chance to prove themself.

When thinking about the law of influence as an educator that is looking to be more of a risk-taker, these characteristics are going to give one greater leeway in trying things and influencing others to try things. For example, let's say that a teacher wants to try a new flexible seating configuration in their classroom. If that teacher kept to themself in the classroom and did not work with their colleagues, never sought out advice or conversations with their supervisor(s), and simply asked for money to buy new classroom furniture without a plan or any evidence to support why they want to incorporate flexible seating, how likely is their principal going to approve of the funding for the venture? Risk will be better supported by their supervisors and colleagues if a person has put in the work by demonstrating character, building relationships, continuously learning, and using their experience to exact positive change on their classroom, school, and community.

Maxwell also cites the law of process as an important aspect of leadership. He points out that worthwhile ventures do not happen overnight and to be successful, a great deal of work and patience needs to be put in over a long period of time. Maxwell refers to the career of Theodore Roosevelt as a prime example of the law of process, demonstrating that Roosevelt challenged himself both physically and mentally to overcome obstacles throughout his life on his road from a sickly boy to president, even holding boxing matches at the White House during his time as president and continuously reading and learning until he died with a book under his pillow (Maxwell 2007, pg. 33).

As educators, we are faced with challenges daily and while we wish we could snap our fingers and improve the home lives of our students, raise test scores, and graduate 100% of students that walk the halls of our buildings, we know that it is not that easy. That's why we need to trust the process and take risks along the way. The mantra of "this is the way we have always done it" rarely improves the most important aspects of our duties as educators and as the saying goes, we need to crack a few eggs to make an omelet. Trying new things in the name of school and classroom improvement and trusting the process instead of giving up at the first sight of struggle is imperative if we are going to truly improve and raise student achievement.

Maxwell's law of intuition is another important aspect of leadership that can be applied to education. And in his words, intuition is hard to define because it is not concrete (Maxwell 2007, pg. 89). Intuition is something that relies on facts, on instincts, and other things like relationships that have been built with others. Decisions can be made based on facts alone, they can be made on gut feelings, or they can be using a combination of facts and feelings.

When I was a football coach, I was the special teams coordinator in charge of kickoff, kickoff return, field goals/extra points, and punting. My head coach gave me freedom to make the calls without consultation so long as a decision I made did not come during crucial times of the game that could potentially spell disaster, such as running a fake punt on our own five-yard line when we were down a touchdown late in the game. As a result of this freedom, I worked with my student-athletes relentlessly on what many would refer to as "trick plays" in addition to the standard practices. In most years, our team would recover at least ten onside kicks. In one game, the other team did not have the ball until we were up 21-0 after I had the team start the game with an onside kick, then proceeded to kick two more after subsequent touchdowns.

Was it risky to start a game with an onside kick, let alone kick three in a row? Absolutely! It could have given the opposing team great field position to start the game and potentially put us down early. However, I studied game film for potential weaknesses. I looked for tendencies from opposing players, such as a front-line blocker turning their back to the kickoff before it was downfield, to find where our kicker could boot a short one and give us a chance for a recovery. Our classrooms are no different. When we know that something needs to be done, we sometimes rely on the facts, such as low scores on an assessment. But other times, we need to rely on our gut in order to try something. Regardless of if a risk is based on fact, feeling, or both, we don't know what the results are going to be, but in order to improve, we need to sometimes take the exit ramp and take the scenic route instead of keeping the wheel straight and working in autopilot mode.

Motivation is a large part of our everyday lives as educators. We can be motivated for a variety of reasons, whether it is because we are naturally motivated to get up each day to go to school and do our best, because we have amazing colleagues and supervisors that push us to be our best, or in the case of some educators, to simply make a paycheck, go home, and count down the days to summer vacation (if you are reading this book, I highly doubt that fall into the latter of these categories). In his book, *Drive: The Surprising Truth About What Motivates Us*, Daniel Pink explores the things that motivate humans to do the things that we do.

According to Pink (2009), humans have always been motivated, but the priorities of motivation have shifted. Thousands of years ago, people were motivated to do things in order to survive. However, after the Industrial Revolution, motivation shifted. For a factory, or society in general, to function efficiently, people needed to be on the same page and a series of carrots and sticks were devised in order to properly motivate people. The thought that if a person did their job well, they would be compensated, or if they did not do their job well resulted in them losing their job worked well, and can still be true, for the most part. The problem is that not everyone is motivated by the carrot and stick approach.

There are a couple of layers to the carrot and stick approach that are applicable to education. First, think about students and students' grades in particular. For many students, they are always striving for the best grade they can get. We have all had that student that has a 99% in a class but comes to us looking for extra credit so they can get to 100%. We also have those students that no matter what carrots and sticks are presented, they simply cannot be motivated to put in the work to improve their skills and demonstrate that they have learned what we are trying to teach them. Even telling them that failing a class could prevent them from graduating on time isn't a motivator to them.

Our colleagues are the same. Some of my colleagues are the ones that are at school two hours before the first bell and stay late before taking more work home. Others are the ones that show up at the contractually obligated time, leave as soon as they can go and rarely take anything home with them. Those that put in the extra hours look at the work as a way to improve their students' achievement, whereas those that don't put in the hours often believe that if they aren't going to benefit directly from those extra hours, such as in the form of extra pay, then they are going to do it.

Motivation in education can also be about support from supervisors and colleagues. If one works with a group of teachers that are always pushing one other to be better, working together to plan lessons and assessments, and work with an administrator that asks what they can do for the individual or the group rather than what the individual or group can do for them, the likelihood that this person is a motivated individual is greater than if the opposite were true and they worked more in a silo without support from others.

Pink himself dove into education and motivation, stating that education's current state is compliance instead of engagement (Pink 2009, pg. 108). He stated that education is based more on control with the intention of compliance rather than giving students and educators the autonomy that leads to engagement. He tied this back to motivation's carrot and stick approach, which worked fine for the repetitive tasks born out of the Industrial Revolution, but something that doesn't work as well in a society that requires people to put forth more effort and be more inquisitive to solve complex problems, problems that require one to be engaged, not just compliant.

So how do we shift classrooms from compliance to engagement? It involves a significant amount of risk. We need to shift from stand and deliver instruction, worksheets, and multiple-choice assessments (and from state mandated testing while we are at it) and teach with a more student-centered approach that relies on demonstration of learning rather than regurgitation of facts and formulas that are only applicable in the moment rather than in the scheme of real life. If you're reading this, you are most likely already a supporter of these concepts. However, like the complicity of motivation that Pink summarized, we need more to be on the same page for it to work. We need to work together to teach better, we need to take risks and share the success and failures of our risks, we need to model risk-taking to inspire others around us to try things. Only then can we shift education from control and compliance to autonomy and engagement.

At this point, perhaps you have taken the words of Maxwell and Pink that inspired me, and you are thinking, "I'm ready!" But perhaps you are still on the fence, with one word that prevents many from trying things: failure. Even thinking about phrases like, "Fail is just a first attempt in learning," doesn't reduce the anxiety of thinking about failing at something. But rather than thinking about a failure as a first attempt in learning, think about it like Brian Aspinall does in his book *Risk Taker*: determination.

Failure in school means a lot of things: do-overs, fixing things, repeating things. Shifting thoughts from failure to determination can mean the same thing but have a more positive ring to it (Aspinall 2020). Think about the stories you have heard about various people and how their determination led to their success, such as Michael Jordan being cut from his junior varsity team in high school, or times in your own life where you were bound and determined to do something, such as the first time I beat Super Mario Bros. on the original Nintendo when I was about ten years old (and how when I lost last Mario, I had to go back to the beginning of the game and do it all over again!). Do you think of Michael Jordan as a failure? Am I a failure because it took me hundreds of hours to finally beat Bowser?

If we are asking our students to be risk-takers and we are taking risks to reach them in innovative ways, let's not look at the bumps in the road as failures. Let's look at them as simple bumps in the road and be determined to succeed. But let us also embrace other characteristics in our road of risk-taking that Aspinall encourages: be unafraid, encourage and embrace change, have courage, and finally, take a risk!

How Has COVID-19 Impacted Risk-Taking?

Since the COVID-19 pandemic's grip on the world came about in March 2020, a lot has changed in many people's views of risk-taking. Teachers were essentially forced to embrace teaching techniques and technology that they were apprehensive or hesitant about prior to schools shutting down. With students participating in school online from home for many places around the world, a whole new set of challenges faced educators, from lack of technology to connect with students, Wi-Fi that was unavailable to many, and engaging students in their home environment, a place where logging into a video conference, turning off the camera and microphone, and disengaging in school was common for many. Teachers had to try a variety of things in attempts to engage their students in ways that they never had to before.

In the short term, risk was something that most embraced, mainly because they had to in order to provide an education for their students. Teaching online via Google Meet, Zoom, Microsoft Teams, or other video programs and assigning work through Google Classroom, Microsoft Teams, Canvas, etc. is a place for teachers to try new things because, frankly, what was it going to hurt? Could it get worse than what education had become during those agonizing weeks and months after schools shut down? Tasks that had been done in class face-to-face or on paper were now replaced with videos (or profile icons when cameras were turned off) and a slew of other tools like Quizizz, Kahoot!, Nearpod, Pear Deck, and many more. And as schools returned to hybrid and in-person instruction, many teachers that had tried these new tools and methods continued to use them.

However, as the pandemic dragged beyond 2020 and into 2021 and 2022, the idea of risk began to shift for many educators. While many continued to try new things to engage students in a world post-COVID, many educators found themselves wondering how much longer they would be able to continue in education. A teacher shortage that had been prevalent for years prior to the pandemic was exacerbated further with teachers resigning en masse to pursue other careers or retire early. Many couldn't or wouldn't wait until the end of the school year, quitting in the middle of a semester. Many expressed that they couldn't wait for things to "get back to normal" so they could get back to teaching how they had done for years prior.

Unfortunately, being an educator is even more challenging now that it was before and there is no returning to what we did before. For many students, they did not see the inside of a school building for nearly a year and a half. The freedom of doing work, taking a break, eating, etc. was taken away when returning to the regimented school day, with many expressing that students "forgot how to do school." And while it was challenging to motivate and engage students during school shutdowns, the same can be said of the return. Because of these challenges, it is even more important that educators embrace risk-taking and make it a part of their lives.

Final Thoughts

Ultimately, whether the results are good or bad, risk-taking makes us better educators and better people if we choose to learn from the results. That lesson that appeared to fall on its face when the technology didn't work or most of the students were not as engaged as you hoped that they would be? If you tried it again, what did you do to adjust it and make it better? That job you took and decided that you were in over your head? How did it make you better in your next position? What lessons did you take from your many mistakes and apply it to a return to the classroom or another role in a different department, office, etc.? Your cross-country move? Did you fall in love with your adopted hometown? Did you move back home after a couple of years? Are you still there, but debating what your next move is because you just aren't sure if you made the right decision? Did you tell a corny dad joke to your class in an attempt to engage them and simply get crickets? Regardless of your answers to any of these questions, realize that you are the person and educator that you are today because of these risks and beyond and apply the lessons that you learned to your future.

After reading these previous few pages, I hope that you have a new sense of risk and what it means to you. I hope that it has given you inspiration to embrace risk more often. I hope that it has given you the tools to analyze a decision more and to analyze the results of a risk with the intention of learning from your experience. I encourage you to not only try new things and learn from them, but also to share with your colleagues, on social media, etc. the good and the bad from your experience. I would love to connect with you to hear your stories of risk-taking! I can be found on Twitter and Instagram (@AndersonEdTech), I write an educational blog at www.andersonedtech.net, I am the co-host of two podcasts, The BeerEDU Podcast with Ben Dickson, and The Podcast by Sons of Technology with Joe Marquez, and as mentioned previously, I am the author of *To The Edge: Successes & Failures Through Risk-Taking*.

Chapter 16
The Impact on Public Education as a Whole

Dr. Lloyd Kilmer

Illustration by Lloyd Kilmer

Introduction

E rnest Hemingway, the preeminent American writer of the twentieth century, gives us direction for the twenty-first century. As a high school English teacher for many years teaching, among other things American Literature, my sophomores and juniors explored the tumult of the several wars, the Great Depression, and emerging American Dominance. Hemingway explored the concept of courage in the face of physical, emotional, and metaphysical danger. There are ways to cope with it. All teachers, professors, administrators, support staff and of course the kids will find their way into the post-pandemic world – a world that will be much different from the one they left in March 2020. Who will make it? Charles Darwin postulated that in the natural world, those species who adapt best to change, survive. Which schools, which systems, which communities will survive?

In a career that spanned four decades in K-12 and higher education across these two centuries, I would subscribe to the adaptation factor. My baptism to teaching was with ninth graders in a short-lived experiment called "Individualized Education." Now it is called "Personalized Education." Students were diagnosed with what they knew and didn't know, and given a set of classroom experiences and paper packets of activities to complete based on the diagnosis. There were three grades of English students in a single pod building, with no walls! My teammate was an experienced but traditional teacher but somehow the synergy worked, and we made progress and had a chaotic good time. The administration fostered a climate of innovation and excellence that provided me with a great start to my teaching career.

Then came a transfer to the high school where the experiment of the day was "Modular Scheduling." There were twenty-one periods per day with almost a collegiate type of schedule of small groups of fifteen students, lab groups of ten to twenty and large groups of 100-150 students. There was time for one on one and small group coaching, teaching, and providing the opportunity to collaborate to put on a good show for the weekly large groups. One of the most memorable was the Amer. Lit., a large group made a presentation on wealth, marketing, and status trademarks to set up the study of *The Great Gatsby*. They were quizzed on trademarks, jingles, and other marketing gimmicks. As the high school was in a relatively wealthy suburb, the students were amazed by how much they were influenced by advertising and the clever symbols and sounds and words that were presented to them non-stop by the media. The technology revolution also hit us at the time bringing the Apple IIE into the tools for teaching! Now our students are awash in the media from hundreds of on-line and off-line sources. How will our twenty-first century kids adapt to media overload and still learn? How will the classroom change to serve the digitally oriented children and teachers?

Innovation in Small to Large Schools

My next assignment was as an administrator, serving first as a Dean of Boys and Department Chair in a suburban high school of 2100 students followed by serving as an assistant principal in a grade seven through twelve building in a small agricultural community outside of the metro area. I learned a lot about connecting with families and community and helping teachers develop. This school was quite traditional in the structure and delivery of education. However, my graduate studies had introduced me to the middle school concept, designed around the unique developmental needs of early adolescents (eleven to fourteen-year-olds); it is a bridge between elementary and high school and advocates meeting the specific needs of all children. The adaptation was to create a "school within a school" with faculty who had the right skills and dispositions to work with middle schoolers. It costs more to organize and support this system and there was resistance within the faculty and community, but the design was strong, and the system adapted to serving this group of students more effectively. In addition, I oversaw discipline for one thousand girls and boys, evaluated half the faculty, attended graduate school, and raised a family. These types of demands were challenging but are not unlike the terrific challenges of the pandemic era. Meeting students and teachers' social-emotional needs is a high priority for all administrators. Perhaps the middle-level approach with teacher-advisors, team planning, and interdisciplinary activities should be brought back not only for middle level but also for high school.

I then moved to the other end of the county to become principal of another seven through twelve building in another small community. The load grew with even more professional responsibility, advanced graduate studies, and the family. This school was even more traditional and needed some system changes as well as updating the curriculum and the quickly advancing technology being implemented in schools. Again, my graduate studies informed me about "Total Quality Management," the system invented by an American but brought to Japan to rebuild decimated industries from WWII. The miracle of Sony, Honda, and Toyota with the quality of their products and relentless customer service changed manufacturing in profound ways. The world adapted to these systems but alas education did not. My dissertation work was driven by the quality maxim of "to meet and exceed the expectations of the customer." Curriculum, personnel, counseling, and facilities ultimately were affected by our TQM pursuit of excellence. The relationship is different in school with students being producers and customers, teachers are coaches and managers, and the community is the ultimate customer.

How would the school meet the needs of the big three customers: higher education, the workplace, and the military? Would the kids and teachers adapt to meeting higher expectations to more with less in a much more competitive world? The response of employers and schools in the Metro Omaha area was to set up partnerships with area manufacturing, retail, and knowledge businesses through a School to Work consortium that spanned the metro area and surrounding communities. As a result of paid summer internships for teachers with companies; the faculty created more authentic classroom experiences which drove higher levels of achievement and were monitored and measured carefully. We followed another TQM maxim that bookends customer expectations with "that which gets measured, gets done." An example of the partnership payoff was the traditional consumer science cooking class that was transformed into a test kitchen using experience gained from a world class food producer. Another was a problem-based activity in geometry calculating the design and volume for packaging at the highest efficiency with the least material for very odd-shaped items inspired by the fast-growing e-commerce industry. At a personal level, one student who was convinced she wanted to be a social worker spent her student internship discovering there is a lot of work done in gathering resources for families and not so much working with them. She decided to explore a new career path. How will our students explore the new careers and work systems emerging in the post pandemic world? Will they adapt to working from home? Will they adapt to a world of jobs that require much different preparation? Will companies adapt to a new relationship with employees?

Teaching, Administration, and Innovation in Higher Education

Finally, I "graduated" from high school and was hired as an educational leadership professor at a regional university in Missouri. This was a school that had already won several awards for Quality at the state level and would later win national awards. This was the right place for me; innovation was the lifeblood of the institution. The Ed. Leadership Department embarked on the then new system of distance learning at multiple sites in the state and neighboring states (pre-Zoom). I once taught school law to five sites simultaneously on the new Iowa Interactive Network. Several of us even packed up and flew to the other side of Missouri on Wednesday nights in the university plane to provide administration classes in a market where no other school offered them. The credo was, wherever at least ten students needed classes, we provided the service, either live or virtually.

When rural districts complained to the State Department in the early 2000s about the lack of math, science, and foreign language teachers, the university and Ed. Leadership Department responded. The Department created an alternative high school certification system design which consisted of recruiting college graduates in small towns, offering a crash course on class management and methods, and providing close internships supported by cameras in the classrooms monitored by faculty who coached the intern. One of the best recruits was a local farmer with degrees in agronomy and land management who agreed to teach biology and chemistry. It worked for him as an extra income stream in the part of the year where the farm demands were less and had great credibility with the students and community.

Finally, what does an urban district like Kansas City do when they start the school year with two hundred open positions (mostly secondary) – you call the university. The program developed by the Department involved recruiting talented undergraduates to participate in an internship with the

KCSD to grow their own teachers. To draw them in, those of us who taught the practicum class to undergrads devised a partnership with a middle and high school in one of the most diverse parts of the city. The three-day mini internship gave them a chance to see the potential and rewards of working in a building with seventy-plus languages and twenty-five different countries represented. One young lady was blown away by an eighth grader from Bosnia who spoke five languages, interpreted in her classes, and helped the principal communicate with families. Later, that young lady signed up for a full semester internship with KCSD excited about the prospects of urban education. While the outside was tough (metal detectors at each door), the inside was welcoming and warm. In the cafeteria each of the kid's countries of origin were proudly represented by a flag. Again, authentic experience was the key. This type of hands-on experience and relationship development will be a key in the future to meet the increased needs to train and deploy teachers in a very demanding employment market.

The final move to Western Illinois was an excellent career move. As a member of the Educational Leadership Dept., now Educational Studies, the faculty provided the training and support to future principals and superintendents and doctoral students. All of my K-12 experience came into play as the Leadership Department started the shift from emphasis on mostly managerial functions to "leadership." Research by Marzano and Reeves started to demonstrate and document what really "worked" in improving school outcomes. The "startup" doctoral program gave the team an opportunity to design coursework and research experiences that were grounded in theory and practice.

Our president was a visionary and gave faculty permission to provide more students over a greater geographical area masters, specialist and doctoral programs. This charge took us from Chicago to Moline to Brown County to Peoria and many other locations. The new instructional television delivery system allowed for multiple sites to receive instruction and faculty many times took to the road to deliver programs on site to support future leaders. We all learned to be doctoral chairs, distance teachers, and researchers. In addition, a new campus was built in the Quad Cities to serve the region with many programs. This provided a chance to serve as the Assistant Dean of the College of Education with programs in counseling, law enforcement, undergraduate and graduate education, and recreation. The mix of urban, suburban, and rural, traditional and non-traditional and Veteran students was exhilarating, and challenging. But the change was manageable.

What will higher education, K-12 and communities do to adapt to the severe teacher shortages, changing education delivery systems and rapidly changing demographics? We will look to those who can display grace under pressure and adapt to change.

Now what?

Hallelujah, there are several vaccines for COVID-19 being deployed widely. All of us are hopeful that this innovation will allow us to reconstruct our lives after the pandemic. However, there are serious disruptions to our educational and business environments that will change this picture. The income and opportunity gap has been exposed to everyone, and that gap is widening.

Disruption One

The schedule, delivery, and the relationships in school for children and adults are now different, both positive and negative. K-12 children have been shuttling between full school to live two days a week and remote three days to remote all the time to packets of worksheets to Google classroom – to finally attending in pandemic pods for homeschooling. Will we find that kids will want to go back to 180 days of 8:00-3:30 attendance sitting at a desk? Will university students want to return to the lecture halls, labs, and seminars of the past? Their schedules have been yanked from under them and their futures clouded as the university copes with its residential and academic disruption.

Ironically, perhaps the evolution of online and distance learning from the university gives us some clues. In the nineties, innovative educational companies started developing online degree programs for degree seeking returning adult learners, place bound learners and learners looking for skill and experience enhancement. The University of Phoenix, Walden University, Kaplan University and many other companies and traditional universities scrambled to fill this demand and develop on-line delivery systems. Some of these institutions were exploitative, some just poorly capitalized and designed, and some evolved into quality alternatives to traditional face-to-face schooling. Other schools developed television-based distance classes to remote sites to expand reach and enrollment. The most recent innovation was the hybrid class mixing on-campus meetings with most of the course work offered online.

Perhaps these are models that can become more permanent options for K-12 schools? However, the university poured resources into teaching professors how to teach at a distance or online and spent hundreds of millions of dollars for electronic platforms such as Blackboard. Will cash strapped K-12 districts have the electronic and technical horsepower and personnel to make this work? Maybe. Dollars that may have been spent for brick-and-mortar investments in the past will give way to more resources being spent on professional development, equity in wi-fi, and hardware access and curriculum revision.

The pandemic has ripped the Band-Aid off the wounds of chronically under-serving students of color and poverty in the basics of education as well the technology of education. The Band-Aid has also come off the wounds of under-serving students in rural areas. "Beyond the Disrupted educational challenges, however, low-income families face an additional threat: the ongoing pandemic is expected to lead to a severe economic recession." Valley High School (NV) Principal Ramona Esperanza says, despite she and her staff working hard to provide a higher quality experience, "I think it's going to take years for them to be able to catch up and that scares me." Valley HS is 66% Hispanic; 16% African American; 8% white and the remainder Asian, Native American and Pacific Islander. "Are we going to lose these kids permanently academically" (Berns, 2020)? On top of these issues are meeting the nutrition and medical needs of the great Clark County's 328,000 students, many of whom live in poverty.

Disruption Two

For adults and children alike, a new psychological phenomenon has cropped up. While counselors and teachers have studied and introduced trauma-informed care to students who by virtue of their environment and/or relationships, experience severe trauma and post-traumatic stress disorder, there is a new version of it - Complex PTSD. The difference is there is no "post." "With CPTSD you're having a traumatic stress reaction, but the trauma is still happening. Unlike a car crash, an assault, or other event, this keeps happening." "The impact of complex trauma is very different to a one time or short-lived trauma. The effect of repeated/on-going trauma – caused by people – changes the brain, and also changes the survivor at a core level. It changes the way survivors view the world, other people and themselves in profound ways" (Capewell, 2020).

In the pre-COVID world almost 60% of US students experienced some form of trauma. More than two thirds of children reported at least one traumatic event by age sixteen (SAMHSA, 2021). This aligns to negative impacts on academic performance and overall health. In my part of Western Illinois and Eastern Iowa, schools have had to adapt to the needs of refugee students who have migrated from many trouble-laden parts of the world. Many of them have lived in refugee camps and have had to move many times across the world. These students have now experienced a "double dose" of trauma. "Nobody has gotten hit with the mental health side of the pandemic worse than kids," said Paul Gionfriddo, the president and CEO of Mental Health America, an organization that supports people with mental illness. "This is an ongoing traumatic event that kids have faced without the perspective of, say, 65-year-olds, who have lived through other kinds of trauma in their lives and have some perspective." (Einhorn, 2021)

However, even these kids can thrive. Schools and agencies have moved many of them up through the Maslow's Hierarchy of Needs Pyramid to a point where they are ready for self-actualization (Cherry, 2021). Several years ago, a group of local trauma-informed teachers brought their high school students to a university conference to read their autobiographical stories to an audience in an authentic performance. The students had written their stories of pain and survival as both a therapeutic and academic exercise and the group of teachers and other health professionals were the audience for these poignant and powerful stories.

Two of these stories illustrate their journey. One young lady from Burma spent time in several camps as violence ran its course through the country. Not only was her journey hard, but she also suffered from a congenital defect in her hips that made movement and walking very painful. After surgery in the US, she now was healthy, happy, and eager to apply to college to become a nurse. A young man from West Africa also spent many years on the run with his family and in camp also presented his story. After learning to read and write he was most appreciative of the opportunities he enjoyed in his adopted country. He wanted to pay back with plans to enlist in the military upon graduation.

How will we support the adults in the school, the parents and grandparents and the children in their recovery to return to some type of school, work and living?

Disruption Three

Schools and other forms of government are experiencing fiscal and structural challenges because of the pandemic. Cities, states, and schools are dependent on taxes as a revenue stream for their budgets. All types of tax revenues such as sales tax, income tax, and government support have been disrupted with the economic recession, and dramatically increased demand for health, first responders, education services, and affordable housing. Thus, far through the end of 2021, there has been minimal provision of support for local and state governments from the federal government. These layers of government are required to operate with balanced budgets that are strained at every turn. In addition, discord during the recent election and a perceived judgment that the government is dysfunctional have created tensions between citizens and their public servants; there is distrust and anxiety.

Schools have tried to handle the spread of disease and danger to faculty and students while trying to provide education and supplemental services. It has not always gone well.

Teachers and staff have well-founded fears about working with students face to face but also are ill equipped to handle virtual education in many cases. Kindergarteners, for instance, cannot learn on Zoom or handle much online activity, even with a lot of supervision. High schoolers are bored and disengaged with the online substitute for live instruction. Parents try to handle a job, child-care, and education all at once – from the kitchen table. This does not often go well.

However, there is a movement to make the hybrid model a more permanent part of K-12 public schooling. "Parent choice is going to drive much of this conversation," Annette Anderson, a Johns Hopkins Professor, advised. "Districts would be wise to think about how they're building out these new options." According to a recent RAND Corp. survey, that process has already begun. Across the country, roughly two in ten district leaders have adopted or are considering their own virtual schools for the long haul.

It will invariably come to finances. "There are funding and equity challenges to consider: If students move out of their home schools and into the new remote schools, for example, funding and staff will follow, a shift that some principals and parents will surely resist." As COVID-19 recedes, as is hoped, there will also likely be a closer look at exactly how remote learning has been for the nation's students, especially those who are most vulnerable." https://www.edweek.org/technology/no-going-back-from-remote-and-hybrid-learning-districts-say/2021/0

Finally, the quasi-home schooling dubbed "pandemic pods" is part of this disruption. Faced with closing schools, rampant spread of the virus and anxiety about the lack of classroom instruction, parents started setting up the pods. Many of these were in affluent large cities such as the Bay Area and Chicago suburbs. Pods were established with trusted families with similar values on safety and educational needs. Parents (paid and volunteer), out of work and retired teachers, and other adults were recruited to run the pods while the parents maintained their work at home schedules. "Parents are increasingly turning to micro schools—very small schools that usually have a specific culture— and learning pods," *The New York Times* noted last month. "Micro schools can be based outside or inside a home, and may or may not be state-approved and accredited. Learning pods are generally ad hoc and home-based, most having been created this summer in response to public school closings." The movement is spreading, "Amidst this chaos, the exodus has been impressive. In their stand-alone form, learning pods are essentially rebranded homeschooling co-ops, with participants counted as homeschoolers. According to a Gallup survey, after years of steady growth, the ranks of homeschoolers doubled this year from 5 percent of all students to 10 percent; traditional public schools saw a drop in enrollment from 83 percent of all students to 76 percent" Liberation Hub, 2020).

Final Thoughts

How will the market and government eventually respond? There will probably continue to be flare-ups of COVID variants that require many of the same restrictions we endured in the past eighteen months. There are many areas of the country that are experiencing severe teacher shortages as the Boomers retire and fewer young people are being trained. There will be more innovative applications of technology to expand educational services and we will get better at delivering them. The stakes are high - failure to effectively compete with other countries will eventually contribute to a decline in the quality of life for students and adults alike. Hopefully young professionals will demonstrate "grace under pressure" and meet the challenge.

Notes

11. Embracing Online Courses

1. Sutton, N. (2021). *Make Professional Development Matter*. EduMatch Publishing.
2. Lieberman, J., & Wilkins, E. (2006) The Professional Development Pathways Model: From Policy to Practice. *Kappa Delta Pi Record*,42(3), 125. https://files.eric.ed.gov/fulltext/EJ738070.pdf
3. Seto, L. (December 2016). Learning from Educator Experiences in a Hawaiian School: Peak Professional Learning and A'o. University of Hawaii at Manoa. https://scholarspace.manoa.hawaii.edu/bitstream/10125/51527/2016-12-edd-seto.pdf
4. Darling-Hammond, L., Hyler, M. E., and Gardner, M. (2017). Effective Teacher Professional Development. Palo Alto, CA: Learning Policy Institute. https://files.eric.ed.gov/fulltext/ED606743.pdf
5. Department of Education Technology. (November 2014). Online Professional Learning Quality Checklist. Section 5. United States Department of Education
6. Means, B., et al. (2009). Evaluation of Evidence-Based Practices in Online Learning: A Meta-Analysis and Review of Online Learning Studies. United States Department of Education   https://www2.ed.gov/rschstat/eval/tech/evidence-based-practices/finalreport.pdf
7. Rabbitt,B., Finegan, J., and Kellogg, N. (October 2019). Research-Based, Online Learning for Teachers. The Learning Accelerator. https://bplawassets.learningaccelerator.org/artifacts/pdf_files/Research-Based-Online-Learning-for-Teachers.pdf

Bibliography

Adobe. (2021, August 23). UI vs. UX Design: The Similarities & Differences | Adobe XD. Ideas. Retrieved July 5, 2022, from https://xd.adobe.com/ideas/process/ui-design/ui-vs-ux-design-understanding-similarities-and-differences/

Aguilar, Elena. Onward. John Wiley & Sons, 2018.

American Association of School Libraries. (2018, Nov. 11). *Definition of an Effective School Library*. American Library Association. Retrieved December 9, 2021 from www.ala.org/aal/advocaacy/resources/statements.

Applegate, K. & Castelao, P. (2012). *The one and only Ivan*. NY, New York: Harper.

Arnett, T. (2021). Breaking the Mold: How a Global Pandemic Unlocks Innovation in K-12 Instruction. *Clayton Christensen Institute for Disruptive Innovation*.

Arp, L., Woodard, B. S., & Harris, F. J. (2003, Spring). Information literacy in school libraries: it takes a community. (Information Literacy And Instruction). *Reference & User Services Quarterly, 42*(3), 215+. https://link.gale.com/apps/doc/A100807864/SUIC?u=char9 7836&sid=bookmark- SUIC&xid=ba30789b.

Aspinall, B. (2020). Risk Taker: Strengthen Your Courage, Blaze a New Trail and Ignite Your Students' Passions. Brian Aspinall.

Association of Illinois School Library Educators. (2018). *Linking for Learning* (4th ed.). Association of Illinois School Library Educators.

Baker, S.K., Fien, F., Nelson, N. J., Petscher, Y., Sayko, S., & Turtura, J. (2017). Learning to read: "The simple view of reading". Washington, DC: U.S. Department of Education, Office of Elementary and Secondary Education, Office of Special Education Programs, National Center on Improving Literacy. Retrieved from improvingliteracy.org

Baer, J., Kutner, M., and Sabatini, J. (2009). *Basic reading skills and the literacy of America's least literate adults: Results from the 2003 National Assessment of Adult Literacy (NAAL) Supplemental Studies (NCES 2009-481)*. National Center for Education Statistics, Institute of Education Sciences, U.S. Department of Education. Washington, DC.

Berman, Sheldon, et al. "The Practice Base For How We Learn: Supporting Students' Social, Emotional, and Academic Development." *NATIONAL COMMISSION ON SOCIAL, EMOTIONAL, AND ACADEMIC DEVELOPMENT*, The Aspen Institute, Mar. 2018.

Berns, D. (2020) How long will pandemic set back our students? Could be years, principal says. *Las Vegas Sun*. Retrieved November 15, 2020 from https://lasvegassun.com/news /2020/oct/20/how-long-pandemic-harm-students-years-principal/

Birsh, J.R. & Carreker, S. (Eds.). (2018). *Multisensory teaching of basic language skills* (4th ed.). NY, New York: Brooks.

Brown University Information Futures Lab. (2022). Information Futures Lab | Where ideas and evidence meet policy and practice. Information Futures Lab. Retrieved July 5, 2022, from https://sites.brown.edu/informationfutures/

Browning, N., Hagle, S., & Boninger, F. (2021). Virtual schools in the U.S. 2021. Boulder, CO: National Education Policy Center. Retrieved [date] from http://nepc.colorado.edu /publication/ virtual-schools-annual-2021

Bueno, C. (2020). Bricks and mortar vs. computers and modems: The impacts of enrollment in K-12 virtual schools. *Computers and Modems: The Impacts of Enrollment in K-12 Virtual Schools (July 3, 2020)*.

Capewell, O. (2020) Because of The Pandemic, People Are Battling A Disorder They've Never Faced Before. Huffington Post, Retrieved December 5, 2020 from https//www.huffpost.com/entry/coronavirus-pandemic-ptsd-mentalhealth-n-5fad6f5ec5b635e9dea0038f?

Casas, Jimmy. *Culturize: Every Student. Every Day. Whatever It Takes*. Dave Burgess Consulting, Inc., 2017.

CASEL. "About Us". *CASEL*. 2021. https://casel.org/about-us/

CAST. (2022, February 8). About Universal Design for Learning. Retrieved July 5, 2022, from https://www.cast.org/impact/universal-design-for-learning-udl

CAST (2018). Universal Design for Learning Guidelines version 2.2. Retrieved from http://udlguidelines.cast.org

Center for Humane Technology. (n.d.-a). Brain Science. Retrieved July 5, 2022, from https://www.humanetech.com/brain-science

Center for Humane Technology. (n.d.-b). Center for Humane Technology. Retrieved July 5, 2022, from https://www.humanetech.com/ Center for Humane Technology. (n.d.-c). Take Control of Your Social Media Use for Well-being. Retrieved July 5, 2022, from https://www.humanetech.com/take-control

Chall, J.S. (1996). *Learning to read: The great debate* 3 ed. Fort Worth, TX: Harcourt Brace.

Chall, J.S. (2000). *The academic achievement challenge: What really works in the classroom*. New York, NY: The Guilford Press.

Chauvin, B.A. (2003) Visual or Media Literacy?, Journal of Visual Literacy, 23:2, 119-128, DOI: 10.1080/23796529.2003.11674596

Cherry, K. (2021) The Five Levels of Maslow's Hierarchy of Needs. *Very Well Mind*. Retrieved March 29, 2021 from https://www.verywellmind.com/what-is-maslows-hierarchy-of-needs-4136760

Child Study Center, Yale School of Medicine. "Comer School Development Program." *Child Study Center: Community Partnerships*, 24 Sept. 2019, https://medicine.yale.edu/child-study/communitypartnerships/comer/.

Cohn, C. (2021) An Impossible Position, AASA School Administrator, Number 8, volume 78, pg 24

Common Core State Standards Initiative. (n.d.). English Language Arts Standards | Common Core State Standards Initiative. English Language Arts Standards. Retrieved July 5, 2022, from http://www.corestandards.org/ELA-Literacy/

Consortium on the School-Based Promotion of Social Competence. (1994). The school-based promotion of social competence: Theory, research, practice, and policy. In (Eds.), Stress, risk, and resilience in children and adolescents: Processes, mechanisms, and interventions (pp. 268–316). New York, NY: Cambridge University Press.

Contreras, S. and Carr, N. (2021) Equity Warriors, School Administrator, Number 3, Vol 78, pg 22

Croft, A., Coggshall, J., Dolan, M., Powers, E. (2010). *Job-embedded professional development: What it is, who is responsible, and how to get it done well.* [Issue Brief]. National Comprehensive Center for Teacher Quality.

Cruise-Roberson, G. Douglas, O., Fiarman, S. (2021) Examining Systems and Self for Racial Equity, School Administrator, Number 3, Vol 78, pg 16

Cruz, M. C. (2019). *Writers read better: Nonfiction.* Thousand Oaks, CA: Corwin.

Darling-Hammond, L., Hyler, M. E., Gardner, M. (2017). *Effective teacher professional development.* Palo Alto, CA: Learning Policy Institute.

Department of Education Office for Civil Rights (US DE OCR, 2021). *Education in a pandemic: The disparate impacts of COVID-19 on America's students.* https://www2.ed.gov/about/offices/list/ocr/docs/20210608-impacts-of-covid19.pdf

Department of Education Technology. (November 2014). Online Professional Learning Quality Checklist. Section 5. United States Department of Education

Deshler, D.D. & Schumaker, J. B. (2006). *Teaching adolescents with disabilities: Accessing the general education curriculum.* Thousand Oaks, CA: Corwin.

Dewey, J. (1986). Experience and education. In the Educational Forum. Taylor & Francis Group, 50 (3), 241-252.

Dewey, J. (1997). Experience and Education, New York: Touchstone

Duckworth, S. (2018). How to Sketchnote: A Step-by-Step Manual for Teachers and Students. Elevate Books Edu.

DuFour, Richard. Learning by Doing: A Handbook for Professional Learning Communities at Work. Bloomington, Ind: Solution Tree, 2006.

Education Trust. (2021). The Importance of Strong Relationships. Retrieved from: https://edtrust.org/wp-content/uploads/2014/09/The-Importance-of-Strong-Relationships- as-a-Strategy-to-Solve-Unfinished-Learning-March-2021.pdf

Einhorn, E. (2020) COVID is having a devastating impact on children – and the vaccine won't fix everything. *NBC News.* Retrieved January 10, 2021 from https://www.nbcnews.com/news/education/covid-having-devastating-impact-children- vaccine-won-t-fix-everything-n1251172

Ferren, M. (2021). Remote Learning and School Reopenings: What Worked and What Didn't. *Center for American Progress.*

Finley, T. (2014, February 19). Common core in action: 10 visual literacy strategies. Edutopia. Retrieved July 5, 2022, from https://www.edutopia.org/blog/ccia-10-visual-literacy-strategies-todd-finley

Fullan, Michael, and Joanne Quinn. *Coherence: The Right Drivers in Action for Schools, Districts, and Systems.* Corwin & Ontario Principals' Council, 2016.

García, Ofelia, et al. *The Translanguaging Classroom.* Caslon, 2016, p. 20.

Georgiou, Bacchiochi, & Soland, (2021). COVID-19's impact on children's reading scores: Data trends and complementary interview. *The Reading League Journal*, 2(2), 34-39.

Gretes, F. (2013, Aug. 12). *School Library Impact Studies: A Review of Findings and Guide to Sources.* Gretes Research Services. Retrieved November 30, 2021 from https://cdn.ymaws.com/www.palibraries.org/resource/collection/FAAEA358-CF27-4976-   889B-2F95015B1AEC/School_Libraries_at_Risk_-_Library-Impact-Studies.pdf.

Goodman, K. (1986). *A parent/teacher guide to children's learning: What's whole in whole language.* Portsmouth, N.H.: Heinemann.

Goodman, K.S., Shannon, P., Freeman, Y.S., & Murphy, S. (1988). *Report card on basal readers.* Katonah, NY: Richard C. Owen.

Gordon, R. (2021) Growing Up in Poverty, Principal Leadership, Volume 21, Number 9, pg. 34

Guilliam, J (2020), Seats at the Table. Mexican American School Boards Association

Harris, B. (2020). *Critical condition: The students the pandemic hit hardest homework in aMcDonald's parking lot: Inside one mother's fight to help her kids get an educationduring coronavirus.* New York, NY: The Hechinger Report.

Harris, M.L., Schumaker, J.B. & Deshler, D.D. (2008). *Learning strategies curriculum: The mapping strategy.* Lawrence, KS: Edge Enterprises.

Hattie, J. (2009). Visible learning: A synthesis of over 800 meta-analyses related to achievement. London: Routledge.

Haycock, K. (2001) Closing the Achievement Gap. Educational Leadership, Volume 58, Number 6, pg. 11

Herold, B. (2021). No Going Back From Remote and Hybrid Learning, Districts Say. *Ed Week.* Retrieved January 8, 2021 from https://www.edweek.org/technology/no-going-back-from-remote-and-hybrid-learning-districts-say/2021/0

Holley, A. (2021) Championing Equity and Diversity, School Administrator, Number 3, Vol 78, pg 43

Honig, B. (2001). *Teaching our children to read: The components of an effective, comprehensive reading program.* Thousand Oaks, CA: Corwin.

Honigsfeld, Andrea, and Maria G. Dove. *Collaborating for English Learners.* Second, Corwin Press, 2019, p. 18.

Huffman, J. B., & Hipp, K. K. (2003). Reculturing schools as professional learning communities. Lanham, MD: Rowman & Littlefield.

Illinois State Board of Education (n.d.) *Subsequent Teaching Endorsements.* Illinois State Board of Education. Retrieved December 24, 2021 from https://www.isbe.net/Pages/Subsequent-Teaching-Endorsements.aspx.

Institute of Museum and Library Services. (n.d.). Museums, Libraries, and 21st Century Skills: Definitions. Retrieved July 5, 2022, from https://www.imls.gov/issues/national-initiatives/museums-libraries-and-21st-century-skills/definitions

International Literacy Association (2020). *Meeting the COVID-19 challenges to literacy instruction: A focus on equity-centered strategies* [Literacy leadership brief]. https://literacyworldwide.org/docs/default-source/where-we-stand/ila-meeting-the-COVID-19-challenge.pdf.

International Literacy Association (2019). *Right to supportive learning environments and high-quality resources* [Research brief]. Newark, DE: Author.

Irwin, V., Zhang, J., Wang, X., Hein, S., Wang, K., Roberts, A., York, C., Barmer, A., Bullock

Mann, F., Dilig, R., and Parker, S. (2021). *Report on the condition of Education 2021* (NCES 2021-144). U.S. Department of Education. Washington, DC: National Center for Education Statistics. Retrieved from https://nces.ed.gov/pubsearch/pubsinfo.asp?pubid=2021144.

Jackson, C. and Dibinga, O. (2021) Social Justice Training to combat inequities, Principal Leadership, Volume 22, Number 2, pg. 36

Jamestown Education (1989). *Timed readings*, 3 ed. Chicago, IL: McGraw-Hill.

James-Ward, C., Pierce, C. and Tapia, J. (2021) Reimagining Education using Pandemic Resources, Volume 22, Number 2, pg. 42

Kafele, B. (2021), The Equity & Social Justice Education. ASCD

Kim, Y. G. & Snow, C. E. (2021). The science of reading is incomplete without the science of teaching reading. *The Reading League Journal*, 2(3), 5-13.

Kluth, P. (2017). Do You See What I Mean? Visual Literacy Supports for Students with Disabilities. Reading Rockets. Retrieved July 5, 2022, from https://www.readingrockets.org/article/do-you-see-what-i-mean-visual-literacy-supports-students-disabilities

Kotter, J.P. (2008), *A Sense of Urgency*, Harvard Business School Press, Boston, MA.

Kotter, J.P. (1996), *Leading Change*, Harvard Business School Press, Boston, MA.

Kouzes, James M., and Barry Z. Posner. *The Leadership Challenge*. 4th ed., Jossey-Bass A Wiley Imprint, 2017.

Kovalik, S. & Olsen, K. (1994). *ITI: The model, integrated thematic instruction* 3 ed. Kent, WA: Susan Kovalik & Associates Distributed by Books for Educators.

Li, J. (1997). Buber's View of Teacher-Student Relationship and Its Enlightenment, Journal of The Northwest Normal University (Social Sciences). 34(1). 9-14. doi:10.16783/j.cnki.n-wnus.1997.01.003.

Liberation Hub. (2020) Bureaucrats Declare War on Learning Pods. They'll lose. *Libertarian Hub*. Retrieved February 10, 2021 from https://reason.com/2020/11/04/bureaucrats-declare-war-on-learning-pods-theyll-lose/

Lieberman, J., & Wilkins, E. (2006) The Professional Development Pathways Model: From Policy to Practice. Kappa Delta Pi Record,42(3), 125. https://files.eric.ed.gov/fulltext/EJ738070.pdf

Lopatovska, I. (2016), Engaging young children in visual literacy instruction. Proc. Assoc. Info. Sci. Tech., 53: 1-5. https://doi.org/10.1002/pra2.2016.14505301101

Lynch, M. (2019, February 28). Teach Your Students Visual Literacy. The Edvocate. Retrieved July 5, 2022, from https://www.theedadvocate.org/teach-your-students-visual-literacy/

Maxwell, J. C. (2007). The 21 irrefutable laws of leadership: Follow them and people will follow you. New York, NY: HarperCollins Leadership.

Means, B., et al. (2009). Evaluation of Evidence-Based Practices in Online Learning: A Meta-Analysis and Review of Online Learning Studies. United States Department of Education https://www2.ed.gov/rschstat/eval/tech/evidence-based-practices/finalreport.pdf

McFarland, J., Cui, J., Rathbun, A., and Holmes, J. (2018). Trends in high school dropout and completion rates in the United States: 2018 (NCES 2019-117). *U.S. Department of Education. Washington,* DC: National Center for Education Statistics. Retrieved from http://nces.ed.gov/pubsearch. Media literacy, 105 ILCS 5/27-20.08, Sec. 27-20.08 (2021). https://www.ilga.gov/legislation/ilcs/fulltext.asp?DocName=010500050K27-20.08.

Merriam-Webster. (n.d.). Library. In *Merriam-Webster.com dictionary*. Retrieved December 22, 2021, from https://www.merriam-webster.com/dictionary/library.

Merriam-Webster. (n.d.). Media. In *Merriam-Webster.com dictionary*. Retrieved December 21, 2021, from https://www.merriam-webster.com/dictionary/media.

Metros, Susan E. (2008) The Educator's Role in Preparing Visually Literate Learners, Theory Into Practice, 47:2, 102-109, DOI: 10.1080/00405840801992264

Moats, L.C. (2020). *Speech to print:language essentials for teachers* 3 ed. Baltimore, MD: Brooks.

Moats, L.C. (2020). *Teaching reading is rocket science, 2020: What expert teachers of readingshould know and be able to do.* Washington, D.C.: AFT.

Moats, L.C. & Tolman, C. (2009). *Language Essentials for Teachers of Reading and Spelling (LETRS): Spellography for Teachers: How English Spelling Works (Module 3)* 2 ed.Boston: Sopris West.

Molnar, A. (Ed.), Miron, G., Barbour, M.K., Huerta, L., Shafer, S.R., Rice, J.K., Glover, A., Roy Norris, E. D., & Teacher, I. Bridging the distance: Remote learning best practices and the LRSD.

Muhammad, Anthony. *Transforming School Culture: How to Overcome Staff Division.* Solution Tree Press, 2009.

N.A. (2004). Professional Development Strategies: Professional Learning Communities/Instructional Coaching. *Annenberg Institute*

National Assessment of Educational Progress (NAEP, Multiple Years). https://nces.ed.gov/nationsreportcard/reading/

National Center for Educational Statistics (2017). *Program for the international assessment of adult competencies (PIAAC).* nces.ed.gov/surveys/piaac/state-county-estimates.asp

National Institute of Child Health and Human Development (NICHD, 2000). *Report of the national reading panel teaching children to read: An evidence-based assessment of the scientific research literature on reading and its implications for reading instruction.* (NIH Pub. No. 00-4754 EXR 001P). Jessup, MD: National Institute for Literacy at EDPubs.

National Child Traumatic Stress Initiative (2021) Understanding Child Trauma. *SAMHSA.gov.* Retrieved November 2, 2021 from NCTSI Infographic (samhsa.gov)

New York Daily News. (2021, Aug. 16). *Meet the warlords See more Bramhall editorial cartoons: bit.ly/3k4Mmee* [Image attached]. Facebook. https://www.facebook.com/NYDailyNews/photos/meet-the-warlordssee-more-bramhall-editorial-cartoons-bitly3k4mmee/10158252601047541/.

Paulson, G. (1987). *Hatchet.* NY, New York: Simon & Schuster.

PBIS Rewards (2021). Building Relationships with Students: 8 Ways to Connect. Retrieved from: https://www.pbisrewards.com/blog/building-relationships-with-students-8-ways-connect/

Pearson, P.D. (1998). Reading instruction that works the case for balanced teaching. New York, NY: Guilford.

Perry, Bruce D. (2020*) Intro to NME Core Slides 2020* [Powerpoint Slides] https://www.neurosequential.com/nme

Pink, D. (2009). Drive: The surprising truth about what motivates us. Riverhead Books, U.S.

Rabbitt,B., Finegan, J., and Kellogg, N. (October 2019). Research-Based, Online Learning for Teachers. The Learning Accelerator. https://bplawassets.learningaccelerator.org/artifacts/pdf_files/Research-Based-Online-Learning-for-Teachers.pdf

Reddick, R. (2021) Racial Equity through Curricular Reform, School Administrator, Number 3, Vol 78, pg 26

Reeves, D. (2020), The E-Squared Solution: Equity and Excellence for every school, Principal Leadership, Volume 20, Number 9, pg 34

Reyes, M. K. K. (2018, November 26). Memes and GIFs as Powerful Classroom Tools. Faculty Focus | Higher Ed Teaching & Learning. Retrieved July 5, 2022

Schawbel, Dan. "Josh Kaufman: It Takes 20 Hours Not 10,000 Hours To Learn A Skill." Forbes. 30 May 2013. https://www.forbes.com/sites/danschawbel/2013/05/30/josh-kaufman-it-takes-20-hours-not-10000-hours-to-learn-a-skill/?sh=5c3c9a0d363d. Accessed 30 Dec. 2021.

Scheurich, J and Skrla, L. (2003), Leadership for Equity and Excellence. Corwin Press

Seto, L. (December 2016). Learning from Educator Experiences in a Hawaiian School: Peak Professional Learning and A'o. University of Hawaii at Manoa. https://scholarspace.-manoa.hawaii.edu/bitstream/10125/51527/2016-12-edd-seto.pdf

Sherman, L. & Ramsey, B. (2006). *The reading glitch: How the culture wars have hijacked reading instruction—and what we can do about it.* Lanham, MD: Rowman & Littlefield Education.

Spina, Carly. *Moving Beyond for Multilingual Learners.* EduMatch Publishing, 2021, p. 22

Stokes, S. (2002). Visual Literacy in Teaching and Learning: A Literature Perspective. Electronic Journal for the Integration of Technology in Education, vol. I, no. 1.

Sutton, N. (2021). Make Professional Development Matter. EduMatch Publishing.

Thomas, K. (n.d.). Kim Thomas, ILSTOY. Kim Thomas ILSTOY. Retrieved July 5, 2022, fromhttps://kimthomasilstoy.com/

Tillmann, Anneliese (2012) What We See and Why It Matters: How Competency in Visual Literacy can Enhance Student Learning. Honors Projects. 9. https://digitalcommons.i-wu.edu/education_honproj/9

Tolisano, S. (2016, November 14). Documenting learning and Media & Visual Literacy. TechLearningMagazine. Retrieved July 5, 2022, from https://www.techlearning.com

Treiman, R. & Altmiller, R. (2021). What science tells us about learning, the nature of written language, reading, and reading instruction. *The Reading League Journal, 2(2), 22-31.*

Treiman, R. & Kessler, B. (2014). *How children learn to write words.* New York, NY: Oxford Press.

University of Birmingham. (2021). LibGuides: Visual literacy: Why Visual Literacy is important. University of Birmingham Library Services. Retrieved July 5, 2022, from https://libguides.bham.ac.uk/asc/visualliteracy

U.S Department of Education, Office of Special Education and Rehabilitative Services (2021). Supporting child and student social, emotional, behavioral, and mental health needs. Washington, DC. https://www2.ed.gov/documents/students/supporting-child-student-social-emotional-behavioral-mental-health.pdf

White, S., Sabatini, J., Park, B.J., Chen, J., Bernstein, J., & Li, M. (2021). *Highlights of the 2018 NAEP Oral Reading Fluency Study* (NCES 2021-026). U.S. Department of Education. Washington, DC: Institute of Education Sciences, National Center for Education Statisitics. https://nces.ed.gov/pubsearch/pubsinfo.asp?pubid=2021026

Wolf, M. (2018). *Reader come home: The reading brain in a digital world.* New York, NY: Harper.

Wolfe, P. (2010). *Brain matters: Translating research into classroom practice,* 2 ed. Alexandria, VA: ASCD.

Woodard, C. (2019). 6 Strategies for Building Better Student Relationships. Retrieved from: https://www.edutopia.org/article/6-strategies-building-better-student-relationships

www.ingramcontent.com/pod-product-compliance
Lightning Source LLC
Chambersburg PA
CBHW050446150626
46551CB00029B/1789